Elements in Publishing and Book Culture
edited by
Samantha Rayner
University College London
Leah Tether
University of Bristol

READING PEER REVIEW

PLOS ONE and Institutional Change in Academia

Martin Paul Eve
Birkbeck, University of London
Cameron Neylon
Curtin University
Daniel Paul O'Donnell
University of Lethbridge
Samuel Moore
Coventry University
Robert Gadie
University of the Arts London
Victoria Odeniyi
University College London
Shahina Parvin
University of Lethbridge

CAMBRIDGE
UNIVERSITY PRESS

CAMBRIDGE
UNIVERSITY PRESS

University Printing House, Cambridge CB2 8BS, United Kingdom

One Liberty Plaza, 20th Floor, New York, NY 10006, USA

477 Williamstown Road, Port Melbourne, VIC 3207, Australia

314–321, 3rd Floor, Plot 3, Splendor Forum, Jasola District Centre,
New Delhi – 110025, India

79 Anson Road, #06–04/06, Singapore 079906

Cambridge University Press is part of the University of Cambridge.

It furthers the University's mission by disseminating knowledge in the pursuit of
education, learning, and research at the highest international levels of excellence.

www.cambridge.org
Information on this title: www.cambridge.org/9781108742702
DOI: 10.1017/9781108783521

First published 2021

A catalogue record for this publication is available from the British Library.

ISBN 978-1-108-74270-2 Paperback
ISSN 2514-8524 (online)
ISSN 2514-8516 (print)

Reading Peer Review

PLOS ONE and Institutional Change in Academia

Elements in Publishing and Book Culture

DOI: 10.1017/9781108783521
First published online: January 2021

Martin Paul Eve
Birkbeck, University of London

Cameron Neylon
Curtin University

Daniel Paul O'Donnell
University of Lethbridge

Samuel Moore
Coventry University

Robert Gadie
University of the Arts London

Victoria Odeniyi
University College London

Shahina Parvin
University of Lethbridge

Author for correspondence: Martin Paul Eve, martin.eve@bbk.ac.uk

ABSTRACT: This Element describes for the first time the database of peer review reports at *PLOS ONE*, the largest scientific journal in the world, to which the authors had unique access. Specifically, this Element presents the background contexts and histories of peer review, the data-handling sensitivities of this type of research, the typical properties of reports in the journal to which the authors had access, a taxonomy of the reports, and their sentiment arcs. This unique work thereby yields a compelling and unprecedented set of insights into the evolving state of peer review in the twenty-first century, at a crucial political moment for the transformation of science. It also, though, presents a study in radicalism and the ways in which PLOS's vision for science can be said to have effected change in the ultra-conservative contemporary university. This title is also available as Open Access on Cambridge Core.

KEYWORDS: academics, evaluation, journals, peer review, publishing

ISBNs: 9781108742702 (PB), 9781108783521 (OC)
ISSNs: 2514-8524 (online), 2514-8516 (print)

Contents

1 Peer Review and Its Discontents

What Is Peer Review and Is It Any Good?

'Peer review' is the system by which manuscripts and other scholarly objects are vetted for validity, appraised for originality, and selected for publication as articles in academic journals, as academic books ('monographs'), and in different forms.[1] Since an editor of an academic title cannot be expected to be an expert in every single area covered by a publication and since it appears undesirable to have a single person controlling the publication's flow of scientific and humanistic knowledge, there is a need for input from more people. Manuscripts submitted for consideration are shown to external expert advisers ('peers') who deliver verdicts on the novelty of the work, criticisms or praise of the piece, and a judgement of whether or not to proceed to publication. A network of experts with appropriate degrees of knowledge and experience within a field are coordinated to yield a set of checks and balances for the scientific and broader research landscapes. Editors are then bound, with some caveats and to some extent, to respect these external judgements in their own decisions, regardless of how harsh the mythical 'reviewer 2' may be (Bakanic, McPhail, and Simon 1989; Bornmann and Daniel 2008; Fogg and Fiske 1993; Lock 1986; Petty, Fleming, and Fabrigar 1999; Sternberg et al. 1997; Zuckerman and Merton 1971).

The premise behind peer review may appear sound, even incontrovertible. Who could object to the best in the world appraising one another, nobly ensuring the integrity of the world's official research record? Yet, considering the system for even a few moments leads to several questions. What is a peer and who decides? What does it mean when a peer approves somebody else's work? How many peers are required before a manuscript can be properly vetted? What happens if peers disagree with one another? Does (or should) peer review operate in the same fashion in disciplines as distinct as neuroscience and sculpture? Particle physics and social

---

[1] As we go on to note, this reductive definition of peer review has come under increasing pressure in recent years as organisations have questioned the reliability of using such judgements for the *selection* of material.

geography? Math and literary criticism? When academics rely on publications for their job appointments and promotions, how does peer review interact with other power structures in universities? Do reviewers act with honour and integrity in their judgements within this system?

Consider, as just one example, the question of anonymity in the peer-review process. Review is meant to assess the work itself, not the authors. If the identity of the authors is available to reviewers, though, then might not they give an easy ride to people they know or allow personal disputes to affect their judgement negatively? It is also possible that radically incorrect work might be erroneously perceived as truthful when it comes from an established figure within a discipline or that bold new and correct work might be incorrectly rejected because it comes from new or unusual quarters (Campanario 2009).

Yet simply removing the names of authors is not itself necessarily a solution. When one is dealing with small pools of experts, this can provide a false sense of security (Fisher, Friedman, and Strauss 1994; Godlee, Gale, and Martyn 1998; Sandström 2009; Wang and Sandström 2015). If a reviewer knows that the work was part of a publicised funded project, for instance, it could be possible to guess with some accuracy the authors' identities. In niche sub-fields, researchers usually all know one another and the areas in which their colleagues are working (Mom, Sandström, and Besselaar 2018; Sandström and Hällsten 2008).

On the other side of this process, what about the identity of the reviewer? Should the authors (or even the readership of the final piece) be told who has reviewed the manuscript (Pullum 1984; van Rooyen, Delamothe, and Evans 2010)? There are arguments for both positive and negative answers to this question. When people are anonymous, they may be more able to speak without constraint. A junior postdoctoral researcher may be *capable* of reviewing the work of a senior professor but might not be able to criticise extensively the work for fear of career reprisals were their identity to be revealed (this also raises the question, though, of what we mean by 'peer'). Yet we also know that the cover of anonymity can be abused. Anonymous reviewers, it is assumed, may be more aggressive in their approach and can even write incredibly hurtful *ad hominem* attacks on papers (Silbiger and Stubler 2019).

Further, how can we tell the standards demanded of a publisher without knowledge of the individuals used to assess the manuscripts? As Kathleen Fitzpatrick notes, conditions of anonymity limit our ability to investigate the review process thoroughly. For 'in using a human filtering system', she writes, 'the most important thing to have information about is less the data that is being filtered, than the human filter itself: who is making the decisions, and why' (Fitzpatrick 2011, 38). It is also clear that errors are only likely to be caught if the selection of peers is up to scratch (although as we note later, there are even some problems with this assumption). Group social dynamics may also affect decision-making in this area (Olbrecht and Bornmann 2010; van Arensbergen, van der Weijden, and van den Besselaar 2014). Gender biases also play a role (Besselaar et al. 2018; Biernat, Tocci, and Williams 2012; Helmer et al. 2017; Kaatz, Gutierrez, and Carnes 2014). Anonymity in the review process, just the first of many concerns, is far more complicated than it might at first appear (for more on this debate, see Brown 2003; DeCoursey 2006; Eve 2013; Godlee 2002; Ross-Hellauer 2017; Seeber and Bacchelli 2017; R. Smith 1999; Tattersall 2015; van Rooyen et al. 1999).

It also seems abundantly clear that the peer-review process is far from infallible. Every year, thousands of articles are retracted (withdrawn) for containing inaccuracies (Brainard and You 2018), for conducting unethical research practices, and for many other reasons (for more on this, see the 'Retraction Watch' site; see Brembs, Button, and Munafò 2013 for a study that found that impact factor correlates with retraction rate). On occasion, this has had devastating consequences in spaces such as public health. Andrew Wakefield's notorious retracted paper claiming a link between the mumps, measles, and rubella (MMR) vaccine and the development of autism in children was published in perhaps the most prestigious medical journal in the world, *The Lancet* (Wakefield et al. 1998). The work was undoubtedly subject to stringent pre-publication review and was cleared for publication. Yet the article was later retracted and branded fraudulent, having caused immense and ongoing damage to public health (Godlee, Smith, and Marcovitch 2011). It is, alas, always easier to make an initial statement than subsequently to retract or to correct it. As a result, a worldwide anti-vaccination movement has seized upon this circumstance as evidence of a conspiracy. The logic uses the supposed initial validation of peer review and the prestige of *The Lancet* as evidence that Wakefield was correct and that he is the victim of a conspiratorial plot to suppress his findings. Hence, when peer review goes wrong, the general *belief* in its efficacy, coupled with the prestige of journals founded on the supposed expertise of peer review, has damaging real-world effects.

In other cases, peer review is problematic for the delays it introduces. Consider research around urgent health emergencies, such as the Zika virus or newly proposed treatments for the 2019 novel coronavirus. Is it appropriate and ethical to wait several days, weeks, or even months for expert opinion on whether this information should be published when people are dying during the lag period? The answer to this depends on the specific circumstances and the outcome, which can only be known after publication. On the one hand, if the information is published, without peer review, and it turns out to be correct and solid without revision, then the checks and balances of peer review would have cost lives. On the other hand, if the information published is wrong or even actively harmful, and there is even a chance that peer review could have caught this, one might feel differently. These are but a few of the problems, dilemmas, and ethical conundrums that circulate around that apparently 'simple' concept of peer review.

In this opening chapter, we describe the broad background histories of peer review and its study. This framing chapter is designed to give the reader the necessary surrounding context to understand the historical evolution and development of peer review. It also introduces much of the secondary criticism of peer review that has emerged in recent years, questioning the usual assumption that the objectivity (or intersubjectivity) of review is universally accepted as the best course of action to ensure standards. Finally, we address the merits of innovative new peer-review practices and disciplinary differences in their take-up (or otherwise). While there are certainly cross-disciplinary implications for our work, it has been in the natural sciences that the benefits and rewards of these new approaches have been most heavily sold.

The Study of Peer Review

Despite the aforementioned challenges, the role of peer review in improving the quality of academic publications and in predicting the impact of manuscripts through criteria of 'excellence' is widely seen as essential to the research endeavour. As a term that first entered critical and popular discourse around 1960 but also as a practice that only became commonplace far later than most suspect, 'peer review' is sometimes described as the 'gold standard' of quality control, and the majority of researchers consider it crucial to contemporary science (Alberts, Hanson, and Kelner 2008; Baldwin 2017, 2018; Enslin and Hedge 2018; Fyfe et al. 2019; Hames 2007, 2; Moore et al. 2017; Mulligan, Hall, and Raphael 2013, 132; Shatz 2004, 1). Indeed, peer review is much younger than many suspect. In 1936, for instance, Albert Einstein was outraged to learn that his unpublished submission to *Physical Review* had been sent out for review (Baldwin 2018, 542). Yet, despite its relative youth, peer review has nonetheless become a fixture of academic publication. This raises the question, though, of *why* this might be the case. For surprisingly little evidence exists to support the claim that peer review is the *best* way to pre-audit work, leading Michelle Lamont and others to note the importance of ensuring that 'peer review processes . . . [are] themselves subject to further evaluation' (Lamont 2009, 247; see also LaFollette 1992). Indeed, there are long-standing criticisms of the validity of peer review, exemplified in Franz J. Ingelfinger's notorious statement that the process is 'only moderately better than chance' (Ingelfinger 1974, 686; see also Daniel 1993, 4; Rothwell and Martyn 2000) and Drummond Rennie's (then deputy editor of the *Journal of the American Medical Association*) 'if peer review was a drug it would never be allowed onto the market' (cited in Richard Smith 2006a, 2010). However, the status function declaration, as John Searle (2010) puts it, of peer review is to institute a set of institutional practices that allow for the selection of quality by a group of empowered, qualified experts (see also Rachar 2016). Peer review as conducted within universities resonates, in many senses, as a type of 'total institution' as defined by Christie Davies and Erving Goffman: a 'distinctive set of organizations that are both part of and separate from modern societies' (Davies 1989, 77) and a 'social hybrid' that is 'part residential community, part formal organization' (Goffman 1968, 22).

Yet research into peer review processes can be difficult to conduct. At least one of the challenges with such studies is that there is always the risk of seeking explanations for the accepted constructions and logics of peer review, rather than recognising the contingency of their emergence. This has not, however, prevented a burgeoning field from emerging around the topic (Batagelj, Ferligoj, and Squazzoni 2017; Tennant and Ross-Hellauer 2019). Certainly, following the influential work of John Swales (1990), an ever-increasing number of studies have examined the language and mood of published academic articles, grant proposals, and editorials (Aktas and Cortes 2008; Connor and Mauranen 1999; Giannoni 2008; Harwood 2005a, 2005b; Shehzad 2015; these examples are drawn from Lillis and Curry 2015, 128). This is not surprising; after all, as van den Besselaar, Sandström, and Schiffbaenker note, '[l]anguage embodies normative views about who/where we communicate about, and stereotypes about others are embedded and reproduced in language' (2018, 314; see also Beukeboom and Burgers 2017; Burgers and Beukeboom 2016). Indeed, a number of existing studies have examined the linguistic properties of peer review reports written by the authors themselves (Coniam 2012; Woods 2006, 140–6; for more, see Paltridge 2017, 49–50).

Yet, as examples of some of the difficulties that hinder the study of these documents, consider that peer-review reports are often owned and guarded by organisations that wish to protect not only the anonymity of reviewers but also the systems of review that bring them an operational advantage – anonymous review comes with several benefits for organisations that are in commercial competition with one another. In particular, and as just one instance, since reviewers often work for multiple publication outlets (that is, the same reviewers can review for more than one journal), the claim of one publisher to have a more rigorous standard of review or better quality of reviewer than other outlets could be damaged were review processes open, non-anonymous, and subject to transparent verification. (It is also clear that top presses can publish bad and incorrect work and that excellent work can appear in less prestigious venues (Shatz 2004, 130).) Further, these organisations often do not have conditions in place that will allow research to be conducted upon peer-review reports. The earliest studies of peer review, therefore, generally used survey methodologies rather than directly interrogating the results of the process (Chase 1970; Lindsey and Lindsey 1978; Lodahl and Gordon 1972). As an occluded genre of writing that nonetheless underpins scientific publication, relatively little is known about the ways in which academics write and behave, at scale, in their reviewing practices.

As another example, an absence of rules and guidelines around owner-ship of peer-review comments certainly contributes to the challenges. The lack of financial incentives in many cases and, therefore, contracts and agreements with reviewers have meant that no clear ownership of reviews has been established (for more on the economics and financials of scholarly communications in the digital era, see Gans 2017; Houghton 2011; Kahin and Varian 2000; McGuigan and Russell 2008; Morrison 2013; Willinsky 2009). In the absence of such statements, it can be assumed that copyright remains with the author of the reports in most jurisdictions. Publishers often do not wish to exert any dominance in this area for fear of dissuading future referees, who can be hard enough to persuade at the best of times. Reviews, therefore, exist in a world of grace and favour rather than one with any clear legal framework. Publishers also benefit from opacity in this domain in other ways. For example, by keeping poor-quality reviews hidden from sight, journals are able to build their reputations on other, less direct, criteria such as citation indices and editorial board celebrity (for more on the occluded nature of peer review, see Gosden 2003). A journal's reviewer database can also provide competitive advantage and bring value to a publishing stable beyond the status of the title itself.

That said, in spite of these difficulties, a substantial number of studies have examined peer review (for just a selection, consider Bonjean and Hullum 1978; Mustaine and Tewksbury 2008; Smigel and Ross 1970; Tewksbury and Mustaine 2012), and it would be a mistake to call the field under-researched, although the methods used are diverse and disaggregated (Grimaldo, Marušić, and Squazzoni 2018; Meruane, González Vergara, and Pina-Stranger 2016, 181). Indeed, Meruane, González Vergara, and Pina-Stranger (2016, 183) provide a good history of the disciplinary specialisa-tions of the study of peer-review processes (PRP) since the 1960s noting that while 'PRP has been a prominent object of study, empirical research on PRP has not been addressed in a comprehensive way.' The precise volume of research varies by the way that one searches, but there appears to be up to 23,000 articles on the topic between 1969 and 2013 by one count – and this does not even include the so-called grey literature of blogs (Meruane, González Vergara, and Pina-Stranger 2016, 181). It is, then, well beyond the scope of this book to provide a comprehensive meta-review of the secondary literature on peer review. The interested reader, though, could consult one of the many other studies that have conducted such an exercise (Bornmann 2011b; Meruane, González Vergara, and Pina-Stranger 2016; Silbiger and Stubler 2019; Weller 2001). Much, although by no means all, of this research has been critical of peer-review processes, finding our faith in the practice to be misplaced (Squazzoni 2010, 19; Sugimoto and Cronin 2013, 851–2; for more positive opinions on the process, see Bornmann 2011a; Goodman 1994; Pierie, Walvoort, and Overbeke 1996). Critics of peer review usually point to its poor reliability and lack of predictive validity (Fang, Bowen, and Casadevall 2016; Fang and Casadevall 2011; Herron 2012; Kravitz et al. 2010; Mahoney 1977; Schroter et al. 2004; Richard Smith 2006b); biases and subversion within the process (Bardy 1998; Budden et al. 2008; Ceci and Peters 1982; Chawla 2019; Chubin and Hackett 1990; Cronin 2009; Dall'Aglio 2006; K. Dickersin et al. 1987; Kay Dickersin, Min, and Meinert 1992; Ernst and Kienbacher 1991; Fanelli 2010, 2011; Gillespie, Chubin, and Kurzon 1985; Ioannidis 1998; Link 1998; Lloyd 1990; Mahoney 1977; Ross et al. 2006; Shatz 2004, 35–73; Travis and Collins 1991; Tregenza 2002); the inefficiency of the system (Ross-Hellauer 2017, 4–5); and the personally damaging nature of the process (Bornmann 2011b, 204; Chubin and Hackett 1990). For instance, and as just a sample, when Rothwell and Martyn (2000, 1964) studied the reproducibility of peer-review reports, they repeated Ingelfinger's assertion that 'although recommendations made by reviewers have considerable influence on the fate of both papers submitted to journals and abstracts submitted to conferences, agreement between reviewers in clinical neuroscience was little greater than would be expected by chance alone.' As another example, more recent work by Okike et al. (2016) unveiled a strong unconscious bias among reviewers in favour of known or famous authors and institutions in the discipline of orthopaedics when using a single-blind mode of review. This casts serious doubt on claims to be able to 'put aside' one's knowledge of an author or to act objectively in the face of conflicts of interest, although in other disciplinary spaces, it has been argued that the definition of merit, as defined in a discipline, is constructed by particular figures and that this identity *should* play a part in the evaluation of their work (Fish 1988). Additionally, Murray et al. (2018, 25) explore the relationship between gender and international diversity and equity in peer review, concluding that '[i]ncreasing gender and international representation among scientific gatekeepers may improve fairness and equity in peer review outcomes, and accelerate scientific progress.'

Special mention should also be made of the PEERE Consortium, which has, in particular, achieved a great deal in opening up datasets for study (PEERE Consortium n.d.). Aiming, with substantial European research funding, to 'improve [the] efficiency, transparency and accountability of peer review through a trans-disciplinary, cross-sectorial collaboration', the consortium has been one of the most prolific centres for research into peer review in the past half decade. Publications from the group have spanned the author perspective on peer review (Drvenica et al. 2019), the reward systems of peer review (Zaharie and Seeber 2018), the links between reputation and peer review (Grimaldo, Paolucci, and Sabater-Mir 2018), the role that artificial intelligence might play in future structures of review (Mrowinski et al. 2017), the timescales involved in review (Huisman and Smits 2017; Mrowinski et al. 2016), the reasons why people cite retracted papers (Bar-Ilan and Halevi 2017), the fate of rejected manuscripts (Casnici, Grimaldo, Gilbert, Dondio et al. 2017), and the ways in which referees act in multidisciplinary contexts (Casnici, Grimaldo, Gilbert, and Squazzoni 2017).

In terms of the language used in peer review reports, work by Brian Paltridge (2015) has examined the ways in which reviewers request revisions of authors, using a mixed-methods approach. Paltridge studied review reports for the peer-reviewed journal *English for Specific Purposes* finding a mixture of implicit and explicit directions for revision used by reviewers, making for a confusing environment in which 'what might seem like a suggestion is not at all a suggestion' but 'rather, a direction' (Patridge 2015, 14), a view echoed by Gosden (2001, 16). Somewhat in contrast to this, though, Kourilova (1998) found that non-native users of English often wrote with an honest, or brutal, bluntness in their reports for a range of sociocultural reasons. While this may come with its own challenges and be painful for authors, such bluntness is far less subject to misinterpretation than hedged attempts at avoiding offence. Comments with such a negative tone can also appear in published book reviews (Salager-Meyer 2001), but these are often more complimentary than behind-the-scenes peer-review reports (Hyland 2004, 41–62). The 'out of sight' or occluded nature of peer review (Swales and Feak 2000, 229) tends, then, to lend itself to more critical judgements.

New Modalities of Peer Review

For some commentators, peer review is the least bad option, and any intervention is only likely to result in poorer outcomes. Others, though, have proposed a range of new methods and operational modes that are designed to address the perceived shortcomings in existing review protocols. Certainly, for the most part, this has taken place within the natural sciences and, as David Shatz remarks, 'the paucity of humanities literature on peer review . . . [is] truly striking', although he is unable to explain why this should be (2004, 4). In this section of this chapter, we outline these new experiments, mostly within this disciplinary space.

Post-Publication Review

The twenty-first century is characterised by what Clay Shirky has famously called 'filter failure' (2008). In the face of an ever-increasing abundance of material – be that scholarly, information, or news – it is apparent that we face severe difficulties in knowing where to spend our scarce attention (Bhaskar 2016; Eve 2017; Nielsen 2011). Various solutions have been posed for how this might be remedied, most of which centre on what Michael Bhaskar calls a culture of 'curation', in which whether by algorithm or by human selection, the 'wheat is sorted from the chaff' (Bhaskar 2016). What it might mean to do so appropriately is, of course, a matter of some contention. Algorithms that surface only mainstream content when we are looking for outliers represent just another problematic case of filter failure, as opposed to any viable solution.

The same problems apply to the scholarly and research literature (Eve 2020). We exist in a world where more is published than it is possible for a person to read, even in almost every niche sub-discipline. Some solutions have taken the algorithmically curated route. Hence, there have been, on the reader side, several attempts to provide automatic summaries of articles, condensing these otherwise large artefacts down into bite-size, digestible chunks ('Get The Research' n.d.; McKenzie 2019; Nikolov, Pfeiffer, and Hahnloser 2018). Yet, we actually exist within a model of digital authorship that R. Lyle Skains (2019) has dubbed 'the attention economy'. It is a model where we only discover material that can float above the otherwise amorphous mass of scholarship. Simply shortening the material itself can help, but it does not resolve the discoverability deficit (Neylon 2010).

This is problematic for scholarly research writing in a way that it is not for, say, works of fiction. While nobody enjoys a badly researched novel, the degree of comprehensiveness required remains considerably less for fiction than for science and scholarship. Writers of historical fiction, for example, conduct research to provide themselves with historically plausible details – appropriate language, modes of transportation, manners of dress, and so on. They seek evidence and descriptions, rather than resolving long-standing debates.

Scientists and scholars, on the other hand, are held to a much higher, though often more narrow, standard. While they are not responsible, as the novelist is, for the construction of an entire world, they are responsible in most cases for the entire range of professional opinion on their topic: what other researchers have found, where they have disagreed, and where the gaps are among them. To conduct new, rigorous research (or even a well-designed replication study), researchers need to have read everything that is pertinent to their topic. Domain mastery is essential and many see the mitigation of this problem as the role of peer review. If there is too much to read and too little time, perhaps too much is being *published*, the reasoning goes. By subdividing fields into topical journals – even if these do, then, mutate into 'club goods', rather than mere subject-based discoverability aids (Hartley et al. 2019; Potts et al. 2017) – and then by limiting the volume that is published, the idea is that researchers have an easy way to keep abreast of their field: simply read that journal.

This model has become untenable and problematic for many reasons. The first is that most high-status journals, which act as poor proxies for quality in institutional hiring and promotion metrics, publish across a range of fields. In addition to monitoring *The Journal of Incredibly Niche Studies*, authors must also regularly check *Nature*, *Cell*, *Science*, *PMLA*, *New Literary History*, the journals of the Royal Society and so on, depending upon their field, all of which publish across sub-disciplinary spaces. In this context, most of the content in these publications will *not* be relevant to a reader who aims to work on a specific project. But they also cannot be dismissed and must be checked. Hence, journal brand does not work well as a filter for subject, even if one believes that it can work as a filter for quality (that is, one might assume – although this assumption is not, in itself, non-problematic – that work published in *Nature* is *good* but it may not be *relevant*) (see Moore et al. 2017).

In light of this discussion, though, we can also query whether the work that is published is necessarily *good*. This is the second problem: given the critiques and failures of peer review to act as a reliably predictive arbiter of quality; if the review system is used as an exclusionary filter, we know that some good work will not be published and that some bad work will nonetheless appear. For although the logic of the system seems sound – the more important and rigorous a work appears to be, when appraised by experts, the more prominence it should be given through publication in a 'top' venue – it is not clear that expert preselection is able accurately to determine, in advance, whether work is important or even correct (Brembs, Button, and Munafò 2013). In this sense, then, peer review cannot act universally well as a filter for quality, either, admitting both Type I (false positive) and Type II (false negative) errors.

What, though, if there were another way of surfacing relevant material that was also good? Given that we only seem to know whether material was accurate and true after the fact, some publications have speculated that post-publication peer review might be a sound way of ensuring that correct material is not excluded, while also seeking expert judgement on the accuracy of work. The basic premise of such systems works as follows:

1. The work is made available online, before a review is conducted;
2. Expert reviews are either solicited or volunteered on the publicly available manuscript;
3. These reviews are either made public or used as evidence to remove the piece from the public record if they are unanimously negative.

One of the challenges with point three is that retractions are less effective than work not entering the public space at all, as we have also seen in the case of the traditionally vetted, but problematic, work by Wakefield. Further, for technical and preservation reasons, retracted articles are not removed but merely marked as retracted. Post review may, if anything, make the problem of fraudulent or incorrect work entering the public record – a major reason for establishing a vetting system in the first place – worse and even more difficult to correct.

Proposals for post-publication peer review arise as a recognition of the fact that we are not very good at determining, ahead of publication, what is important and good. However, it comes with its own challenges. When a publisher seeks a traditional pre-publication review, they could argue that they are conducting a form of due diligence, in which they have done the best they could to ensure the accuracy of material. This could be important in specific biomedical sciences and the applied medical literature, even if we know that peer review has flaws. In a model that uses post-publication peer review, it is not clear that the same could be said. If material is published that then causes harm, it is not clear that a publisher could argue that they had done everything they could to prevent this, even when they do not endorse the material. Further, it is unclear who would take the legal blame here. While authors usually must sign a waiver for negligence due to inaccuracy, publishers are the ones displaying the material and claiming that they add value to the truth of the work. In addition, in many jurisdictions one cannot disclaim negligence for death or injury. Further, if one believes that peer review does do at least some good in filtering out bad material, then it is clear that this model of peer review will be one in which readers would 'have to trek through enormous amounts of junk' to find true material and one in which inundation frustrates truth (Shatz 2004, 16, 25). This is also a type of 'post-truth' system in which, it is claimed, all competing views are equally legitimated: 'flat earth theories now can be said to enjoy "scholarly support"' (Shatz 2004, 16; see also Holmwood 2020).

PLOS ONE, the journal that is the subject of the study to which most of this book is devoted, uses a system of post-publication review with an initial review on grounds of 'technical soundness'. In other words, there is a filtering system of pre-review at *PLOS ONE*, but it is not predicated on novelty, importance, or significance (although reviewers are free to alert editors to the potential significance of work if it is proved to be correct). Rather it is supposed to examine purely whether the experiment was established in a sound fashion and executed according to that plan, whether it is technically sound. Whether or not reviewers actually assess according to these criteria is something to which we will later turn. Whether or not post-publication peer review even actually happens with any regularity is another problematic matter (Poynder 2011, 17).

Most systems of post-publication peer review, such as that piloted at *F1000*, present a 'tick box' mechanism, where readers can easily see the review status on an article. This usually takes the form of marking the work as 'approved' ('The paper is scientifically sound in its current form and only minor, if any, improvements are suggested'), 'approved with reservations' ('Key revisions are required to address specific details and make the paper fully scientifically sound'), or 'not approved' ('Fundamental flaws in the paper seriously undermine the findings and conclusions'). In this way, *F1000* gives clear signals to its readership on the opinions of reviewers towards the material, while not preselecting in advance. This allows for an evaluation of both the article *and* the review process, especially since the reviewer names and comments are publicly available, the subject of the next section.

Open Peer Review

There is little to no standardised consensus on what is meant by the term 'open peer review', even within the self-identifying 'open science' community (Ford 2013; Hames 2014; Ross-Hellauer 2017; Ware 2011). As Tony Ross-Hellauer notes:

> While the term is used by some to refer to peer review where the identities of both author and reviewer are disclosed to each other, for others it signifies systems where reviewer reports are published alongside articles. For others it signifies both of these conditions, and for yet others it describes systems where not only 'invited experts' are able to comment. For still others, it includes a variety of combinations of these and other novel methods. (2017, 3)

Indeed, for Ross-Hellauer, seven types of open peer review are identified in the secondary scholarly literature on the subject:

- Open identities ('Authors and reviewers are aware of each other's identity.')
- Open reports ('Review reports are published alongside the relevant article.')
- Open participation ('The wider community are [*sic*] able to contribute to the review process.')
- Open interaction ('Direct reciprocal discussion between author(s) and reviewers, and/or between reviewers, is allowed and encouraged.')
- Open pre-review manuscripts ('Manuscripts are made immediately available (e.g., via pre-print servers like arXiv) in advance of any formal peer review procedures.')
- Open final-version commenting ('Review or commenting on final "version of record" publications.')
- Open platforms ('Review is facilitated by a different organizational entity than the venue of publication.') (Ross-Hellauer 2017, 7; for an alternative taxonomy, see Butchard et al. 2017, 28–32)

While 'open pre-review manuscripts' were covered in the earlier section on the temporality of review, any of these other areas are up for grabs under the heading 'open review'. As such, we will treat each here in turn.

We have already given some attention to issues of anonymity in review, but one of the definitions of open peer review seeks to make public the names of reviewers, either to authors or to the readership at large. It is worth adding to the previous discussion, though, that a series of studies in the 1990s showed, counter-intuitively, that revealing the identity of reviewers makes no difference to the detection and reporting of errors in the review process (Fisher, Friedman, and Strauss 1994; Godlee, Gale, and Martyn 1998; Justice et al. 1998; McNutt et al. 1990; van Rooyen et al. 1999). Nonetheless, in the early 2020s many venues were experimenting with forms of open or signed reviews, most notably, again, *F1000*, which also provides platforms for major funders such as the Wellcome Trust. Such venues also extend into the 'open reports' category, as it is possible to read the reviews provided by each named reviewer. This comes with a type of reputational benefit to reviewers, surfacing an otherwise hidden form of labour for which credit is not usually forthcoming.

Models of 'open participation' in which anyone may review a manuscript are more contentious, for they might stretch the bounds of the term 'peer' to the breaking point (for more on which, see Fuller 1999, 293–301; Tsang 2013), although some systems such as Science Open require that a prospective referee show they are an author on at least five published articles (as demonstrated through their ORCID profile) to qualify (Ross-Hellauer 2017, 10). It is also the case that such open participation efforts can see low levels of uptake when reviewers are not explicitly invited (Bourke-Waite 2015). That said, there have been extensive calls for greater inter-activity that would replace the judgemental and potentially exclusionary characteristics of peer review with dialogue between researchers but also with a wider community (Kennison 2016). Furthermore, the development of external review framework sites such as *Pubpeer* and *Retraction Watch* have fulfilled a genuine community need for scrutiny of work, *after* it has been published. These are community-run sites, often with anonymous commenting, and so suffer, technically, from the same drawbacks as other open participation platforms. However, several high-profile instances of misconduct have been identified in recent years through such platforms, demonstrating substantial value even as these mechanisms sit outside the mainstream practices of peer review.

Finally, sites such as *Publons*, *RUBRIQ*, *Axios Review*, and *Peerage of Science* offer or have offered independent services whereby reviews can be 'transferred' between journals. In theory, this makes sense; as the same reviewers often work for different publications; behind the scenes, there is a mass duplication of labour in the event of resubmission to a new venue. It is even possible that the same reviewers may be asked to appraise work at a different journal if work is resubmitted elsewhere. In practice, though, this portability poses substantial challenges for journals. For example, one might ask, what is the point of a journal if peer review is decoupled from the venue? If the work has been reviewed, why could it not appear in an informal venue, such as a blog or personal website, and merely point back to the peer-review reports? This would be particularly potent if the names of the reviewers were also available. There are also questions of versioning. Ensuring that it is clear to which version each peer review points is critical in such situations.

New Media Formats

Finally, while it might seem, at first glance, that the media form of the object under review is irrelevant to a review process, this is not the case. Despite debates over the fixity of print (Eisenstein 2009; Hudson 2002; Johns 1998), the fundamentally unfinished and even incompletable nature of interactive, collaborative, and born-digital scholarship poses new challenges for peer review (Risam 2014). For if work continues to go through iteration after iteration, as just one example, how are review processes to be managed, at a point when peer review already appears to be buckling beneath the burden of unsustainable time demands (Bourke-Waite 2015)? Further, one might also consider how new types of output – software, data, non-linear artefacts with user-specific navigational pathways (interactive visualisations, for instance), practice-based work – would fare under conventional review mechanisms (Hann 2019).

Conclusions

Since its rise to prominence in the late twentieth century, peer review has occupied a leading place in the cultural scientific imaginary. It has been enshrined as the gold standard for the arbitration of quality and is often falsely thought to be a timeless element of scientific intersubjectivity. Yet, despite its seventeenth-century or eighteenth-century origins (Butchard et al. 2017, 7; Fitzpatrick 2011, 21) and its evolution to become 'sanctified through long use' (Baverstock 2016, 65), the wide-scale adoption of peer review is nowhere near so old as many people imagine and, as this chapter has shown, there is also much disquiet about its efficacy, accuracy, and negative consequences. This has led to a range of new, experimental practices that attempt to modify the peer-review workflow, changing the temporalities (pre- vs post-), visibilities (open identities vs anonymity), and positional relationalities (at-venue vs portability) of these practices. Given the speed of ascent with which peer review has moved to claim its crown, though, it would not be surprising if another modality of practice could rise as swiftly to supplant it. Surely, though, any new method would also be subject to fresh critique. For none of the mentioned methods is perfect and peer review is likely always to have its discontents.

This leads to the obvious question: in relation to process and procedure, does change actually happen? If changes to processes are mooted, does this lead to substantive change in practices or indeed broader cultural and intellectual change? What opportunities are there to test such questions?

In the remainder of this book, we turn to these questions through a focal lens on the Public Library of Science (PLOS). We present this organisation as a case study in attempted radicalism in peer-review practice and unearth the degree to which it has been successful in initiating institutional change in academia. In Chapter 2, we examine the ways in which PLOS sought to reshape review and the challenges that it faced. We give a background history of the organisation and its mission, which are crucial to understanding PLOS's strategy for change. We also detail the sensitivities of and difficulties faced in studying a confidential peer-review report database and the protocols that we had to develop to conduct this work. We finally look at the overarching structure of the database, detailing how much reviewers write and the subjects on which they centre their analysis.

In Chapter 3 we turn to a set of specific questions around PLOS's supposedly changed practice. In this chapter, we ask whether PLOS's guidelines yield a new format of review; whether reviewers in *PLOS ONE* ignore novelty, as they are supposed to; whether reviews in *PLOS ONE* are more critically constructive than one might expect; how much of a role an author's language plays in the evaluation of a manuscript; how much of a reviewer's behaviour can be controlled or anticipated; and to what extent reviewers understand new paradigms of peer review. The last part of this chapter details our only partially successful efforts to use computational classification methods to 'distant read' the corpus. Finally, in Chapter 4 we turn to an appraisal of the extent to which PLOS has managed to change the standards for peer review in a broader fashion.

As a final note, the subtitle of this book makes reference to 'institutional change in academia' more widely. Isn't it presumptuous to assume that PLOS and its niche crafting of new modalities of peer review can act as a synecdoche for all types of change within academia? Perhaps. Yet PLOS has been incredibly influential. It has grown to house the largest single journal on the planet, and it was founded from a position espousing radical change. We believe, therefore, that valuable lessons can be drawn from PLOS's experience. We now move to set out the background against which these lessons can be taught.

2 The Radicalism of PLOS

A New Hope

We closed the introduction with a set of questions. These can be summarised as follows: given an agenda for new practice, what opportunities are there to observe and critique interventions intended to drive change?

The Public Library of Science (PLOS) can safely be characterised as an organisation that shared the concerns about peer review that we outlined earlier and that has sought to drive such change through a radical approach. Instigated in the year 2000 as a result of a petition by the Nobel Prize–winning scientist Harold Varmus, Patrick O. Brown of Stanford, and Michael Eisen of the University of California, Berkeley, PLOS – or 'PLoS' as it was initialled until 2012 (PLOS 2012) – was originally established with the support of a \$9 million grant from the Gordon and Betty Moore Foundation. The vision here was one of a radically open publication platform in which *PLoS Biology* and *PLoS Medicine*, their two initial publications, would 'allow PLoS to make all published works immediately available online, with no charges for access or restrictions on subsequent redistribution or use' (Gordon and Betty Moore Foundation 2002).

Yet open access to published content, itself a fairly outlandish proposition at the time, was not enough for PLOS. Frustration was growing among the founders and board that peer review was returning essentially arbitrary results. As Catriona J. MacCallum put it, '[t]he basis for such decisions' in peer review 'is inevitably subjective. The higher-profile science journals are consequently often accused of "lottery reviewing," a charge now aimed increasingly at the more specialist literature as well. Even after review, papers that are technically sound are often rejected on the basis of lack of novelty or advance' (2006). PLOS wanted to do something different.

Specifically, in 2006 PLOS established *PLOS ONE* (again, originally *PLoS ONE*), a flagship journal that works differently from many other venues. The peer-review procedure at *PLOS ONE* is predicated on the idea of 'technical soundness' in which papers are judged according to whether or not their methods and procedures are thought to be solid, rather than on the basis of whether their contents are judged to be important (PLOS 2016b). Notably, though, even this definition is contentious: subjectivity is involved in the assessment of whether a methodology is rigorous and sound (Poynder 2011, 25–26). For instance, to understand whether a methodology is suitable, one must not only know and understand its mechanics but also *imagine* potential problems and alternative experiments. Even while the aim of an experimental set-up is to eradicate subjectivity from observation, it takes imagination and subjectivity to create and then to appraise good experimental design. *PLOS ONE* was nonetheless designed to 'initiate a radical departure from the stifling constraints of this existing system'. In this new model, it was claimed, 'acceptance to publication [would] be a matter of days' (MacCallum 2006).

At the time of its inception, this was a fairly radical idea (Giles 2007; The Editors of *The New Atlantis* 2006). Dubbed 'peer-review lite', the mechanism was nonetheless still far from the more innovative, pure post-publication approaches that we earlier described. Instead, it offered a lowered threshold for publication on the grounds that replication studies ('not novel'), pedestrian basic science ('not significant', or otherwise framed as Kuhnian 'normal science'), and even failed experiments ('not successful') should all have their place in the complete scientific record. Of course, one might ask how far PLOS would really be willing to take this. Would a well-designed replication study of the boiling point of water be published? It appears to fulfil the criteria of technical soundness while also replicating a well-known result. We doubt, however, that such an article would, in reality, make it through even peer-review lite.

As it was described at the time, the plan was for *PLOS ONE* to use 'a two-stage assessment process starting when a paper is submitted but continuing long after it has been published'. A handling editor – of which PLOS had assembled a vast pool – could 'make a decision to reject or accept a paper (with or without revision) on the basis of their own expertise, or in consultation with other editorial board members or following advice from reviewers in the field' (MacCallum 2006). The fact that handling editors could make their own judgement internally was indeed particularly controversial (Poynder 2011, 26). This review process was supposed to focus 'on objective and technical concerns to determine whether the research has been sufficiently well conceived, well executed, and well described to justify inclusion in the scientific record' (MacCallum 2006).

PLOS also asserted at the time that 'peer review doesn't, and shouldn't, stop' at publication (for more on this, see Spezi et al. 2018). Although disallowing anonymous commenting and having a code of conduct with civility criteria for reviewers, the idea for *PLOS ONE* was that '[o]nce a paper is in the public domain post-publication, open peer review will begin.' This was explicitly driven by technological capacity. It was an area 'where the increasing sophistication of web-based tools [could] begin to play a part' and PLOS's new partnership with the TOPAZ platform at the time drove the capacity for post-publication review (MacCallum 2006). In this sense, the radicalism of PLOS was pushed in part by technological capacity – a technogenetic source made 'possible because some of the limitations and costs of traditional publishing begin to go away on the Internet' (Poynder 2006a). It was also fuelled, though, by the social concerns about peer review, its (lack of) objectivity, and its relative slowness.

Critics further pointed out, though, that the broad scope of *PLOS ONE*, coupled with its high acceptance rate, could be construed as a *revenue model* for the organisation (Poynder 2011, 9). This was one of the main concerns of an economic situation that rested upon the acceptance of papers for a revenue stream: that it might introduce a perverse incentive to accept work. For those with greater faith in conventional peer review, the experiment in peer-review lite was a cynical economic means by which PLOS could cross-subsidise its selective titles, while propounding an ethical argument about the good of science.

In addition to its culture of radical experiment, *PLOS ONE* is, further, an interesting venue as, unlike many other journals, it has a long-standing clause that makes reviews available for research, provided that the research in question has obtained internal ethical approval (PLOS 2016a). And this is where we step in. PLOS provided us with a database consisting of 229,296 usable peer-review reports written between 2014 and 2016 from *PLOS ONE*. While the two-year period gap does contain potential for heterogeneity of policy to cause challenges for analysis, the relatively short time span should, we hope, provide some coherence between analysed units. There were other reports in this database, but the identifiers assigned to them made it impossible to group these reports by review round and so these data were discarded. We wanted to know the following: How have the radical propositions that led to the creation of *PLOS ONE* affected actual practices on the ground in the title? Do PLOS reviewers behave as one might expect given the radicalism on which *PLOS ONE* was premised? And what can we learn about organisational change and its drivers?

As we have already touched upon, papers in *PLOS ONE* span various disciplinary remits, albeit mainly in the natural sciences (where the majority of research into peer review has already found itself focused (Butchard et al. 2017). 'From the start', wrote MacCallum, '*PLoS ONE* will be open to papers from all scientific disciplines.' This was because, it was believed, 'links' of commonality 'can be made between all the sciences': an interesting argument that stops short of asserting that this might also apply to humanistic inquiry (2006). Varmus, indeed, conceived of *PLOS ONE* as 'an encyclopedic, high volume publishing site' across disciplines (2009, 264). As an early staffer at *PLOS ONE* put it, the general view was that 'science subjects developed in a pretty arbitrary way. The boundaries have effectively been imposed as a consequence of the way that journals work, and the way that universities are structured', and *PLOS ONE* was designed, from the outset, to counter such disciplinary siloing (Poynder 2006b). This multidisciplinarity yields opportunities but at the same time also creates evaluative challenges (Collins 2010). Indeed, we must acknowledge early on that our study will be unable to draw discipline-specific conclusions, even while it may be able to speak generally across a relatively broad remit.

While it is unlikely, then, that a large-scale, mass review of peer-review practices across the academic funding and publishing sectors will emerge at any point in the near future, in the descriptive portions of this book, we report on our access to the *PLOS ONE* review corpus and thereby take the smaller step of interrogating a very large dataset that focuses only on the components of peer review concerned with technical soundness and that is ethically cleared for this type of research project. Specifically, in this chapter we describe the data-handling protocol, data-handling risks, and high-level composition of the database, our own aspects of 'technical soundness'. We then move to outline the content types of the reports according to a coding taxonomy that we developed for this exercise and that was used to attempt to train a neural-network text classifier. Finally, we report on the stylometric properties of the reports and the correlations of different language use with recommended outcome.

The Peer Review Database and Its Sensitivities

Securing this database of peer-review reports meant accepting restrictions on its future use and on the extent to which the underlying dataset would need to remain private – a delicate matter to negotiate when one is working in a field of 'open science'. Reviewers have an expectation that their reviews will be used in confidence within the review process and that they can remain anonymous. However, referees agree as part of the PLOS review process that their contributions may be used for research purposes:

> In our efforts to improve the peer review system and scientific communication, we have an ongoing research program on the processes we use in the course of manuscript handling at the PLOS journals. If you are a reviewer, author or editor at PLOS, and you wish to opt out of this research, please contact the relevant journal office. Participation does not affect the editorial consideration of submitted manuscripts, nor PLOS' policies relating to confidentiality of authors, reviewers or manuscripts.
>
> Individual research projects will be subject to appropriate ethical consideration and approval and if necessary individuals will be contacted for specific consent to participate. (PLOS 2016a)

In order to minimise the risks of identification of referees from any analysis conducted (and associated reputational risks to PLOS, authors, and reviewers), our protocol required removal of all identifying data prior to release from PLOS to the project team. The project team never held email addresses or names of referees and all records that relate to submissions or publications in the relevant PLOS journals from any member of the project team were removed from the corpus by PLOS prior to the transfer of the dataset to the team. Where a project member was an academic or professional editor, rather than a reviewer, we did not consider that this posed a risk of reidentification of confidential information. We note that Cameron Neylon was an academic editor for *PLOS ONE* from 2009–12 and a PLOS staff member from 2012–15 but played no editorial role over the latter time period. Sam Moore worked at PLOS from 2009–12 and on *PLOS ONE* specifically from 2011–12.

The dataset was treated as sensitive and analysed only on project computers running the latest distribution of Ubuntu Linux using hard disks encrypted with the crypto-luks system and a minimum key-length of thirty characters. Backups were stored on two non-co-located computers with encrypted hard drives and data were never transferred via email, cloud storage, or other insecure online transmission mechanisms, instead using the secure copy facility (scp) using RSA key-based authentication. Data were only accessed by the researchers charged directly with actual analysis and with Martin Paul Eve or Daniel Paul O'Donnell as their direct supervisor. Other members of the project team had access to summaries that included snippets of representative text. The original dataset was destroyed at the end of the project and unfortunately cannot be shared. To obtain the original dataset, third-party researchers would need to contact PLOS directly. As a consequence, useful data sharing on this project is extremely limited in scope and relates only to compositional matters without any original citation. This, of course, causes substantial challenges for those who wish to replicate and/or verify our findings, and we regret that we are unable to be of much help here. Further, citation of the reports in this article are restricted to generic non-identifying statements and to versions of statements that are either redacted or have had their subject matter replaced or made synonymous. In this way, though, we are able to comment on the ways in which reviewers write and behave, without compromising anonymity and without linking any report to a final published or rejected article.

How Much Do Reviewers Write?

An initial fundamental quantitative question that can be asked of the database is the following: How much do peer reviewers write per review? This is an important question because it bears on the extent to which peer review is a gatekeeping mechanism as against a mechanism for constructive feedback. It takes very few words to say 'accept' or 'reject', but many more to help an author improve a paper. With PLOS's early radicalism and belief that peer review could be a positive force in the new context, it was hard to know what to expect in terms of volume. Figure 1 plots the character counts of reviews in the database and shows a strongly positive skewed distribution peaking around the 2,000 to 4,000 character bands. This is approximately 500 words per report as the most common length (depending on the tokenisation method that is used to delimit words).

There are some significant outliers within this distribution (clear from the very long tail of Figure 1). The mean character count for reports (with an attempt to exclude conflict of interest statements) is 3,081. The median character count is 2,350. The longest report in the corpus, however, is 90,155 characters long, or just under 14,000 words; in all likelihood, this is longer than the article on which it comments (a study showed that for medical journals the mean length of article is 7.88 pages, or roughly 2,000–4,000 words at 250–500 words per page (Falagas et al. 2013)). The second-longest review is 59,946 characters, or approximately 5,000 words. Indeed, at the upper end of the distribution among those reviewers whose reports are voluminous, there appears to be roughly an inverse proportionality to rank in the frequency table. (That is, the first report is twice the length of the second, etc.)

However, some anomalies are masked by the apparent simplicity of this visualisation. For instance, one might assume that second-round reports, where a reviewer appraises whether or not a set of revisions has been accepted, would fall at the shorter end of the spectrum with a stronger positive skew. In our manual-tagging exercise, however, we often found substantive comments in subsequent rounds: indeed, reviewers frequently apologised for introducing additional criticisms in second- and third-round reviews that were not picked up in the original. In the overall amalgamation, we pulled together all sets of comments by the same reviewers on the same manuscript into single documents. Hence, Figure 1 gives a misleading picture of the corpus shape.

A more accurate way of classifying this is perhaps only to look at the first round of review. This distribution of first-round-only reports can be seen in Figure 2.

Plotting the first-round reviews as opposed to the general corpus makes little difference to the overall distribution pattern of the length of reviews. In general, most peer-review reports at *PLOS ONE* are less than 2,351 characters

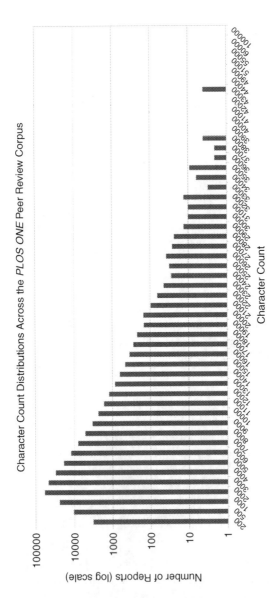

Figure 1 Character count frequency distributions across the *PLOS ONE* peer-review database

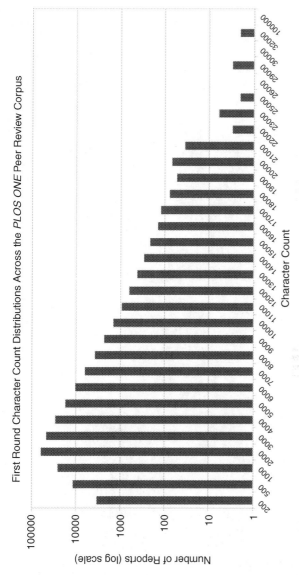

First Round Character Count Distributions Across the *PLOS ONE* Peer Review Corpus

Character Count

Number of Reports (log scale)

Figure 2 Character count frequency distributions across the *PLOS ONE* peer-review database, first-round reviews only

long and the addition of comments appraising whether revisions have been made, as in Figure 2, does not significantly affect the skew. These findings correlate with previous studies of the peer-review process, which found average report lengths to range from 304 to 1,711 words in other disciplinary spaces (Bolívar 2011; Fortanet 2008, 30; Gosden 2003; Samraj 2016). Of course, other studies have concluded that the length of report is not proportional to its quality, when measured by the 'level of directness of comments used in a referee report' (Fierro et al. 2018, 213). An initial glance at the quantity written, though, shows no difference in practice to more conventional journals.

The higher bound for the average length of peer-review reports that we found in a multidisciplinary database has several consequences. For one, it may be indicative of an uneven distribution of length of report between disciplinary spaces. That is, some disciplines may have greater expected norms for the length of report that must be returned to be considered rigorous. At a time when peer review is thought to be growing at an unsustainable rate (Bourke-Waite 2015), this may have different consequences in those disciplines where much longer reports are expected. Indeed, the labour time involved in conducting a peer review inheres not just in the length of the submitted artefact that must be appraised – although, superficially, it is quantitatively more effort to read a monograph of 80,000 words than an article of 2,000 words – but also in the expected volume of returned comments and the level of analytical detail that is anticipated by an editor both to signal that a proper and thorough review has been conducted and to ensure the usefulness of the report. To more accurately appraise the potential strains on the peer-review system, we would urge publishers with access to report databases to make public the average length of their reports by disciplinary breakdown to help disaggregate our findings.

What Do Reviewers Write?

To understand the composition of the database and to communicate these findings in a way that does not cite any material directly, we undertook a qualitative coding exercise (specifically domain and taxonomic descriptive coding (McCurdy, Spradley, and Shandy 2005, 44–45)) in which three research assistants (RAs) collaboratively built a taxonomy of statements derived from the longer reviews. Two of the research assistants were native English speakers based in London in the United Kingdom (Gadie and Odeniyi), although we note that the policed boundary of 'native' and 'non-native' speakers comes with both challenges for the specific study of peer review and postcolonial overtones (Lillis and Curry 2015, 130; see also Englander 2006). The third research assistant is an L2 English speaker based in Lethbridge in Canada (Parvin) with significant social scientific background experience, including with this kind of coding work. Eve and O'Donnell oversaw coordination between the research groups.

The goal of our coding exercise was to delve into the linguistic structures and semantic comment types that are used by reviewers, following previous work by Fortanet (2008). This would allow us to disseminate a description of some of the peer-review database without compromising the strict criteria of anonymity and privacy that the database demanded.

Qualitative coding techniques are always inherently subjective to some degree (Merriam 1998, 48; Sipe and Ghiso 2004, 482–3). Indeed, as Saldaña notes, there are many factors that affect the results of qualitative coding procedures:

> The types of questions you ask and the types of responses you receive during interviews (Kvale 1996; Rubin and Rubin 1995), the detail and structuring of your field notes (Emerson, Fretz, and Shaw 1995), the gender and race/ ethnicity of your participants – and yourself (Behar and Gordon 1995; Stanfield and Dennis 1993), and whether you collect data from adults or children (Greene and Hogan 2005; Zwiers and Morrissette 1999). (2009, 7)

We mitigated some of the language, race, and gender problems by ensuring diversity among the coding and research team. As just one instance of this across one identity axis, without Parvin's input, we would have been confined to a British English anglophonic perspective, a stance that matches the profile of neither PLOS authors nor their reviewers. The triplicate process of coding that we undertook – in which each RA worked at first individually but then regrouped to build collaborative consensus among the group on both sentiment and thematic classification – also helped to construct an intersubjective agreement on the labels assigned for each term. Bormann et al. (2010, 499) also used such a triplicate system. The downside of this approach is that, clearly, we traded accuracy for volume. It is also possible that a different group of coders would have used different terms, and part of our coding exercise involved a process of synonym checking. Such partial and subjectively situated knowledges are, however, an essential and well-recognised part of post-structuralist social-scientific studies, and we acknowledge explicitly our active involvement in the shaping and building of such knowledges (Crotty 1998; Denzin 2010; Haraway 1988).

There are also debates as to the quantity of material that should be coded (Saldaña 2009, 15). We opted to use our RAs' time to work initially on the richer reports, as a preliminary survey of the database did not reveal any types of statement in the shortest reviews that were not present, in some form, in the longer entries. Once the initial taxonomy had been constructed from the tagging of the longest reviews, we then took a random sample of reports from around the median character count length with the number of documents tagged determined by the funding constraints on the time of the RAs. This resulted in 78 triplicate tagged reports, consisting of 2,049 statements. The coding process resulted in the development of a taxonomy of statements found within the *PLOS ONE* review database. At the broadest level these pertained to the following:

- the 'field of knowledge' to which the statement referred
- 'references to data'
- 'section analyses'
- comments on 'omission'
- comments on 'methodology'
- comments on 'expression/language'

Each of these categories had a range of specific sub-tags, which are shown and explicated in Table 1.

In addition to coding against the taxonomy to categorise statements, each statement was also assigned a sentiment score (again negotiated among the three coders). The sentiment scale used ran from −10 (strongly

Table 1 The taxonomy of statements built for the Reading Peer Review project from the *PLOS ONE* database.

High-Level Category	Fine-Grained Category	Explication
Data	Data	A reference to results and/or data.
Data	data-commentary	A description of or commentary upon data, for instance, a reference to a chart's legend.
Data	Interpretation	Extrapolation from data. This category can overlap with data analysis/treatment.
Data	Analysis/treatment	How data are treated after collection. This includes data analysis and statistical analysis. It can also refer to secondary data (sets).
Data	Presentation	Includes reference to data display. Also includes comments on formatting, size of tables, redundancy of images, visibility of images, and size of the images.
Field of Knowledge	(Knowledge) Statement	A statement that the reviewer makes (about fact or community agreed notions). Does not apply to the reviewer paraphrasing the original article. Relates to knowledge claims by the reviewer and/or authors.

Table 1 Cont.

High-Level Category	Fine-Grained Category	Explication
Field of Knowledge	Information for author(s)	Statements that indicate a reviewer's subjective opinion, for example, 'I consider it appropriate to . . . '
Field of Knowledge	Positioning	Reference to ways in which/to what extent the authors position concepts/ideas in relation to others. Can also imply/require the Literature tag (see following).
Field of Knowledge	Literature	Explicit reference to secondary literature. Negative sentiment score in this category refers to misinterpretation or misrepresentation of literature, or lack of relevance of references employed.
Field of Knowledge	Revision	A comment on whether revisions have been made. A positive sentiment score in this category indicates revisions met while a negative means the opposite. This category also includes corrections and reference to subsequent/previous revisions.
Field of Knowledge	Holistic revision	Reviewer signals a range of issues to be fixed through revisions (referring to multiple categories).

Field of Knowledge	Fallibility	Instances where the reviewer admits they may not be correct in their opinion/criticism or admits inadequacy of and uncertainty around judgement.
Field of Knowledge	Tone	Tone of reviewer exhibits bias against non-Western submission/language (patronising). Tone of reviewer exhibits *ad hominem* attack on author or team of researchers. Also used to denote overly familiar personal register/tone. Awarded appropriate sentiment score if tone implies praise or critique of manuscript.
Field of Knowledge	Potential/significance	A remark upon the significance of findings/data/results/work. This also includes the potential of contribution to knowledge or research; references to reproduction of experiments. Also used to flag poor scholarship and auto-plagiarism via a lack of novelty. Note that this category of 'significance' should *not* be a criterion used for judgement of admission within the *PLOS ONE* ecosystem.
Expression	(English) Language	Reference to use of English, languages other than English, native/non-native speakers.
Expression	Typographical errors	Reference to surface-level errors, including grammatical errors. Lack of consistency denotes strongly negative sentiment. Trivial typos are low sentiment score. Comments on punctuation are attributed using this tag.

Table 1 Cont.

High-Level Category	Fine-Grained Category	Explication
Expression	Expression	Communicative quality – coherence of style and academic/scientific register. Choice of language. Rewording. Definitions of terms/acronyms.
Expression	Terminology	Use/deployment of subject-specific terminology. Can refer to accessibility of terms.
Expression	Cohesion	Comments on linkage between sections of paper in terms of correlation, structure, and organisation.
Expression	Style	Comments on adhesion to house style.
Expression	Citation	Referencing and citation practice; includes lack of appropriate citation.
Expression	Summary	When a reviewer summarises or signals a section of paper. Also used as a form of transition before critique. Includes quotations from original text, including title.
Expression	Transition	A transitive statement which makes no reference to the manuscript. Includes notes to editors.
Methodology	Methodology	Broader approach to methods adopted. Also refers to rationale, justification, or basis for research. Ethical issues/concerns.

Methodology	Statistics	In general and/or explicit reference to statistics including statistical tests. Explicit reference or use of statistical tests such as Analysis of Variance (ANOVA), Student's T–Test, Pearson, correlation coefficients, Mann Whitney (package).
Methodology	Experimental design	Reference to a series of experiments, hypotheses, sample size, control groups, parameters, data collection tools, inferential/ descriptive statistics, correlation, data modelling.
Methodology	Method	Refers to the description of method, including procedures, techniques, and discussion of advantageous alternatives.
Methodology	Limitations	Discussion of limitations.
Omission	Implied omission	Implies that something is missing without explicitly stating it.
Omission	Omission	Explicitly states that something is missing.
Omission	Accuracy	Comments on the accuracy of (data) description (& definitions). Can refer to factual or descriptive inaccuracy. Can also refer to (lack of) precision.

Table 1 Cont.

High-Level Category	Fine-Grained Category	Explication
Omission	Elaboration	Request for more detail, information, clarification, or precision. Different to omission in the sense that omission is about something that isn't there at all whereas this tag calls for supplementation.
Omission	Argument/ analysis	Missing discussion of data/results.
Omission	Ambiguity	Reference to clarity, vagueness. Can connote positive (as clear, well worded, etc.) as well as negative sentiment. Instances where something is unclear to the reviewer.
Omission	Argument	Pertains to clarity of argument – exposing point of view. Distinct from 'argument/analysis' in that it deals with literature. Can also refer to the phrasing of an argument. Negative sentiment can refer to redundant or unconvincing argument. Explicit reference to logic or logical can imply this category. Also refers to the coherence of an argument. Claims implying criticism/ agreement.

Omission	Implied criticism	Used for tagging questions from reviewers. Negative meaning/critique implicit. For instance, 'Would this manuscript benefit from X?'
Section	Outcome	Publishability and suitability of results/data/findings. Relates to publishability of specific paper. Usually with reference to the admissibility criteria of *PLOS ONE*.
Section	Overarching comment	Used for tagging comments that broadly apply to the whole manuscript.
Section	Conclusion	Reference to the results of interpretation and/or analysis. Can also refer to results/findings. Reference to implications of results. Also refers to limitations of study.
Section	Abstract	Reference to the work's abstract.
Section	Appendix	Reference to an appendix in a work.

negative) to +10 (strongly positive) with zero (0) denoting a neutral statement. Certainly, sentiment was, at first, the most contentious element of the coders' practice with little agreement among readers. By the end of the process, reviewers found themselves broadly in agreement on sentiment markers with little negotiation required.

An interesting phenomenon that demonstrates some of the limitations of our sample size can be seen in the fact that no statements in our taxonomy pertain to ethics and Institutional Review Board procedures (rather than to the ethics of peer review itself (for more on the latter, see de George and Woodward 1994; reprinted in Shatz 2004)). This is not the case in the corpus as a whole, where reports contain notes expressing diverse sentiments such as '[t]he description of the human research ethics and informed consent process is confusing. Was the research protocol reviewed and approved by an institutional review board (IRB)? If yes, which one?'; 'I have sincere reservations about the authors [*sic*] lack of independent review by an ethics committee'; '[t]hus, review by an ethics board is not needed'; and 'an ethics statement is required in the method section.' While these statements would have been tagged as remarks upon 'expression' and 'omission', they would also have been marked as pertaining to ethics had we encountered any such reports in our tagging exercise. This is important since some reviewers dubbed ethics problems as major concerns with certain manuscript submissions, such as a lack of ethical clearance for work upon vertebrates or cephalopods, one of *PLOS ONE*'s ethics criteria. There are several clear reasons for this. The first is that ethical issues in PLOS policies only apply to a subset of articles and, therefore, only a subset of the random sample. Second, *PLOS ONE* editorial staff screen major ethics issues before assigning papers to academic editors and so we would expect that in the subset of papers for which ethics is relevant, many issues may already have been cleared with authors before the work is sent to peer review.

On the other hand, there were occasionally also statements that merely confirmed that ethics procedures had been followed: '[t]he research meets all applicable standards for the ethics of experimentation and research integrity', for instance. Although reviewers are asked, explicitly, to consider ethical issues in any paper in a separate question, it is notable that our sample did not find any statements on this matter. This could be interpreted to mean that the 'missing' statements on ethics in our sample indicate implicit assent that all ethical matters have been satisfactorily addressed. However, a sociology of absences means that it remains important to continue to pay attention to what might be expected but is not found (Santos 2002). For an important point that informs all of our analysis herein is that *PLOS ONE* editors attempt to screen for policy matters before sending to peer review in any case. This is meant to ensure that work that is not in line with PLOS's publishing policy and could not be published anyway is not sent to reviewers. Such work is incredibly hard to investigate; nonetheless, it sits as an invisible substrata to the reports that are visible.

In the next chapter, we turn to what we can learn about reviewing practices under supposedly radical conditions, and the extent to which this institutional policy can be seen as a driver of academic practice.

3 New Technologies, Old Traditions?

At the end of our year-long coding project, we had tagged 2,049 statements across 78 reports in triplicate consensus. While this constitutes a small proportion of the total dataset, the specific reports were selected using a computational random number generator to ensure that our results came from across the spectrum of review types and represented accurately the underlying database. This chapter details the composition and congruence of the reports that we studied. We also attempt to show whether or not our findings match those made by others in different journal spaces.

More specifically, this chapter aims to appraise whether reviewers in *PLOS ONE*, a journal with radical criteria for peer review, behave in radical ways or stick to tried-and-tested norms. In other words, our investigation here is into the difficulties of organisational change in academia. What does it take, we ask, to change practices? Are policies enough? Is technology sufficient? Or are there broader and deeper social requirements?

Did PLOS's Guidelines Yield a New Review Format?

In line with existing studies on the commonality of report structures and the 'moves' within them (Bornmann 2011b, 201; Gosden 2003; Paltridge 2017, 39–40), which we here confirm, most reviewers for *PLOS ONE* begin their reports with a summary of the manuscript on which they have been asked to comment. That is, reports open by describing the contents of the paper with statements such as 'this manuscript investigates the relationship between t-cells and inflammatory markers in rheumatoid arthritis.'

Indeed, the strongest structural homophily between reports emerges in the opening gambits: sixty-eight of the seventy-eight (87 per cent) reports that we studied contained a summary statement within the first six sentences of the reviews. Of the ten reports that did not contain a summary within the first six sentences, four (40 per cent) were second-round reviews (appraisals of revisions that just cut to the chase), and four (40 per cent) contained at least one summary statement somewhere later in the report. In other words, only six (7.7 per cent) of the reports that we examined contained no statement summarising the research work on which the reviewers were commenting. Such statements usually restate the aim of the paper under review.

In broad terms, these restatements appear to serve three purposes. First, they demonstrate that the reviewer has read the manuscript and can concisely summarise its subject to the editor. This serves a legitimation function in demonstrating the reviewer's understanding of the paper (and that the reviewer has done the required reading) but also as a check on the quality of the paper as a communicative instrument. Of course, this can also be a delegitimation function should a reviewer inaccurately summarise a paper – a good example of an instance where the editor may wish to discard or ignore the contents of a report. In fact, this is evidence for the need for continuing editorial oversight of peer review and a demonstration of an occasion where simply relaying the verdict or accepting the opinion of reviewers is insufficient to conduct a proper review. In pre-review modes, though, this can lead to timing frustrations. If an author has waited a long time for reports to be returned and one of these reports is then shown to be based on a misreading of the paper, it may be necessary to seek an additional reader, leading to further delays to the process.

Second, such statements confirm intersubjectively between the editor and reviewer that they are speaking of the *same* manuscript, a way of ensuring that reports do not become confused between submissions. Although, we presume, rare in the age of comprehensive technological workflow management solutions, anybody who has ever used email can identify with the mortifying sensation of having attached the wrong file. By summarising the manuscript at the very beginning of the report, reviewers give the editor a clear and easy way of checking that no administrative oversight has compromised the review process. This is perhaps a reflection of the review report as a genre that is internalised and continually rehearsed with every review; that is, it is so common to read reviews with summary statements at the beginning that academics assume that all reviews require them.

Third, and finally (while also being linked to the first function), such a restatement of the paper's intent serves as a self-offered check of the reviewer's understanding and fitness to review. This differs slightly from the previous points, although it also carries a legitimation function. It works more as a conditional check that states 'if you accept my interpretation of this paper, then you should accept my verdict as follows.' This *hermeneutic* statement thereby gives the editor much greater room for interventionist manoeuvre if they believe that the reviewer has read the paper from a different disciplinary or sub-disciplinary standpoint. This differs from a factually incorrect statement – 'this paper is about X' – and is usually of the form 'however, if we take Smith and Smith's 2006 results into account, then surely there is a problem with X.' Approximately 20 per cent of the reports that we examined contain statements in which reviewers admit to their own fallibility in the appraisal of the piece under discussion; hence, this third category is important.

Indeed, despite the legitimation function detailed above, in eleven (16.2 per cent) of the examined reports that contain an early summary (and in a total of fifteen (19.2 per cent) examined reports), reviewers also admit their own lack of knowledge or understanding ('fallibility'). Such expressions of self-fallibility varied in their composition. In some cases, this took the form of an implicit and conditional criticism of the communication of the work: 'If I'm understanding the construction of [studied phenomenon]'. In other cases, such statements were warnings to the editor that the reviewer did not feel entirely competent to appraise the work, sometimes followed by a conjunctive adverb ('but' or 'however') to legitimate continued comment on the piece: 'I am not an expert in this field, but . . .'; 'I am not an expert. . . . However'; 'Unfortunately, I cannot comment on [redacted] aspects.' That such statements are widely present indicates that reviewers do not always believe that they are being assigned work that they are able to evaluate. Of course, as research is niche and specialised to particular laboratories, it may be that there is no reviewer in the world who would be totally competent to appraise a piece of work; hence, every reviewer has the potential to share the opinion that they are out of their depth. That said, in only one instance did a reviewer decline to comment entirely on these grounds: 'Unfortunately, the current reviewer is not an expert in the analytical methods used to analyze and characterize the [subject matter] highlighted in this manuscript to give an appropriate review.' We note, though, that other reviewers may have declined invitations on the ground that they were unqualified to comment and that the statement we found was only one of *partial fallibility*. That is, in this instance, the reviewer was simply noting that they could not comment on a particular aspect of the paper rather than the manuscript in its entirety. This may emphasise the importance of using multidisciplinary review teams, including dedicated statisticians. Again, though, this amplifies the labour and time required as well as overburdening statistical reviewers.

On occasion, we tagged instances of such 'hedging' from reviewers as admissions of fallibility. For example, when asking for specific reruns of experiments, terms such as 'perhaps' or 'probably' indicated a level of uncertainty in the recommendation that could lead to such a classification. While there is no universally agreed upon definition of 'hedging' (Crompton 1997; Hyland 1996, 1998, 2000, 2004; Myers 1989; Nash 1990; Prasithrathsint 2015; Salager-Meyer 1994), previously it has been considered as a strategy for politeness (for instance, Brown and Levinson 1987; Dressen-Hammouda 2013; Fernández 2005; Held 2010; Spencer-Oatey and Franklin 2009; Tang 2013; Varttala 2001) with cross-cultural and gender differences in usage (Coates 2013; Hinkel 2005; Scollon and Scollon 2001). In academic writing, hedges imply 'that a statement is based on plausible reasoning rather than certain knowledge' (Hyland 1998, 4), allowing the reader either to become complicit in accepting such a statement or to contest it (Kim and Lim 2015). Again, such hedging in review statements gives the editor lateral freedom to accept or decline a review's perspective. It also gives the author of the paper the opportunity to argue back against the report. Sometimes, reviewers apologise to editors and authors in their reviews, with one report saying 'sorry for a rather unstructured list of too many comments in the attached pdf', admitting fallibility of the organisation of their recommendations. From time to time, such self-appraisals were related to comments on language where the reviewer admits not to speak the language of the paper as their first language or not to know of the linguistic appropriateness of a certain way of writing: 'I am not a native speaker myself'; 'I am not sure that sentences can be started with numeric values or abbreviations.' Interestingly, given anecdotal reports that non-native English speakers are judged more harshly *by* peer reviewers (that is, peer reviewers often see the language as a block to an actual evaluation of the science), it is unclear whether editors take *reader reports* written by non-native English speakers less seriously. It is also true that editors may be non-native English speakers.[2]

This all coheres to paint a picture of reviewer uncertainties that nonetheless act as functional elements of the peer-review system. Reviewers' admissions of fallibility are not simply statements of a factual inability to comment but also play a part of the discursive dynamics of negotiation between reviewers and editors. Occurring in one in five papers, such statements are often conditionally hedged to allow for flexibility in review processes. Of course, this is itself a rhetorical strategy, daring the author or editor to question the judgement of the external reviewer ('I am not sure that sentences can be started with X . . . *are you*?'), while still leaving open the possibility of error. Such statements of fallibility are a good example of the ways in which peer review, when conducted behind the scenes, is a delicate social negotiation, rooted in language practices and communities of practice (Lave and Wenger 1991), with their own expected rules of behaviour and linguistic codes.

In many ways, this finding is not unexpected: *PLOS ONE* asks reviewers to comment on the technical soundness of manuscripts and, for the reasons listed earlier, reviewers have a relatively standard set of legitimation moves in which they can establish their competence to comment and to identify the manuscript. These elements do not disappear under PLOS's criteria for review. Further, the delicate negotiation of reviewer authority continues in the new peer-review environment of *PLOS ONE*, hence the persistence of hedging and of reviewer admissions of fallibility.

Do Reviewers in PLOS ONE *Ignore Novelty?*

Reviewers for *PLOS ONE* frequently comment on the novelty of the papers that they are reviewing, but they do not usually remark upon

---

[2] Puebla and Dunbar (2018) note both that '*PLOS ONE* has a large editorial board with academics from 97 countries' and that 'a large share of the decisions issued are made by Academic Editors based in the United States, Canada, the United Kingdom and Australia – high-income, majority native English-speaking countries' expressing a view that a diversity of editorial voices is important to the quality of the peer review process for the journal.

reproducibility. This is important, as previous work has shown that reviews expressing concerns about a 'lack of originality' were 'likely to be associated with rejection' (Turcotte, Drolet, and Girard 2004, 549). Thus, although the review criteria of *PLOS ONE* are set at a strict boundary of 'technical soundness' and we expected that reviewers would understand this, sixty out of the seventy-eight reports that we tagged (77 per cent) commented either positively or negatively on (and, on some occasions, both positively *and* negatively upon different aspects of) the potential, novelty, and significance of the paper under review. Thirteen (21.7 per cent) of these assertions around originality and significance explicitly used the term 'novel' or 'novelty' in the coded statement, for instance, 'the findings presented are both novel and interesting'; 'the novelty and impact of the current study is low'; 'furthermore, [redacted] has already been shown to influence [redacted] ([redacted reference]) limiting the novelty of this manuscript'; 'there is essentially no novelty in the findings'; 'the novelty of [redacted] is rather low'; 'while the paper is well written and easy to follow, its current shape seems not close to publication, mainly due to lack of novelty.' On one occasion, a reviewer asked explicitly for revisions in which the authors should describe the novelty of the paper: 'the novelty and significance of the study should be clearly described in the Introduction.'

There are three explanations for this. The first is that at least part of the *PLOS ONE* review process *does* request that reviewers comment on the significance, novelty, or importance of the work, albeit not as a criterion for acceptance but rather to assist the editors in highlighting work – after publication – that reviewers believe merits especial attention. Most instances of commentary of novelty in our sample, however, treated this as a positive or negative attribute and used this appraisal within the review as an evaluation criterion, rather than as guidance markers to editors, as part of what Stefan Hirschauer has called the 'reciprocal observations of judgments that complement and compete, control and court one another' during the peer-review process (2010, 74). A second explanation is that when authors remark on the novelty or significance of a portion of their work, they are signposting to the reviewer that this is an important part of the paper – and reviewers' comments reflect this back. That is, within a limited time economy, authors' own remarks upon what is 'new' or 'significant' serve to guide the reader's attention. Finally, though, such statements often appear to indicate, as the third explanation for this phenomenon, that the quest for significance is so ingrained in academic reviewing culture that even when asked specifically not to comment on originality, significance, or novelty, reviewers cannot help themselves.

Such comments on originality and significance stand in contrast to the goals of *PLOS ONE*. As Adam Eyre-Walker and Nina Stoletzki have shown, scientists are poor at evaluating whether a paper will go on to have significant effects (2013). Several studies have also shown that work that went on to achieve high recognition and status could equally well have been rejected at earlier or later parts of significance-based peer-review processes and fared poorly as a benchmarking measure of career success (Azoulay, Zivin, and Manso 2011; Calcagno et al. 2012; Campanario 2009, 1993, 1996; Campanario and Acedo 2007; Ceci and Peters 1982; Costello 2010; Fang, Bowen, and Casadevall 2016; Gans and Shepherd 1994; Lindner and Nakamura 2015; Meng 2016; Nicholson and Ioannidis 2012; Pagano 2006; Siler, Lee, and Bero 2015; Weller 2001). While there is some evidence that reviewers find greater consensus in distinguishing non-acceptable from acceptable work (that is, reviewers find agreement in work that should *not* be published) (Cicchetti 1991; Weller 2001), debates around the roles of novelty and significance in gatekeeping processes continue to rage and, as noted, appear thoroughly embedded within academic expectations and norms. It takes an incredibly long time for things to change. Indeed, given the ongoing prevalence of comment on novelty and significance in the *PLOS ONE* review corpus, there may be some truth to Max Planck's adage about the pace of change in academia. Perhaps science really does advance 'one funeral at a time' (Azoulay, Fons-Rosen, and Graff Zivin 2019).

Hearteningly for the goals of *PLOS ONE*, though, we did encounter reports where reviewers remarked unfavourably upon claims for novelty within the paper (that is, not remarking that a paper's novelty was poor but rather chastising authors for making their *own* claims for novelty): 'the study is novel, but is that necessarily important?' 'the authors make much ado about the fact that the study is the first of its kind, but is it better to be first or to make an important contribution?' and 'I am concerned about the author's insistence on the uniqueness of this study.' On occasion, reviewers praised the modesty of authors, noting that they 'make reasonable and humble claims about the finding with a well-balanced explanation of the limitations of the study'.

In fact, statements on novelty are occasionally used to ask authors to temper their claims: 'while I recognize that this is a novel study, the rhetoric that is being used to sell the message is a little extreme.' Such remarks on novelty, then, are appropriate within the criteria set by *PLOS ONE* when used to ensure that authors do not overstate their claims. There is thus a complicated relationship between significance and soundness that editors have to navigate and a simple edict that 'reviewers should not remark on novelty' is neither appropriate nor sufficient. These, though, were few and far between and not found systematically in the reports that we examined. Of course, without the manuscripts themselves, we cannot appraise how often such criticisms arise compared with how often claims for novelty are made in the respective *PLOS ONE* papers on which the reviews were conducted. It is also the case that *PLOS ONE* editors have the ability to overrule the comments of reviewers that violate policy, such as those on novelty. This applies at both the academic editorial and staff/managing editorial levels. Hence, even if reviewer behaviour has not changed 'under the hood', it is possible that the *outcomes* of the review process are changed.

Given also that one of the goals of *PLOS ONE*'s review criterion of technical soundness is to ensure reproducibility and replication, we were interested to see how often these phenomena were mentioned. There has been much debate in recent years over the fact that most publications do not value replication and reproducibility as conditions of admittance, for a variety of reasons (Aldhous 2011; Goldacre 2011; Lawrence 2007; Lundh et al. 2010; Nosek, Spies, and Motyl 2012; Rothstein 2014; Wilson 2011; Yong 2012a, 2012b, 2012c, 2012d), but we note that, in theory, *PLOS ONE* will publish such work. Of the seventy-eight reports that we studied, only three (3.8 per cent) mentioned reproducibility in their feedback. That said, reviewers commented with great frequency both on matters of experimental design and on methodological aspects. Among the seventy-eight reports coded, forty-four (56.4 per cent) commented on the design of the studies they were reviewing, while fifty-four (69.2 per cent) remarked upon the methods used. Comments on method, though, were overwhelmingly negative, with only three (3.8 per cent) of the reports we studied remarking favourably upon this aspect. The 'experimental design' category fared little better, with only six (7.7 per cent) of the reports that we studied commenting positively upon the way that experiments were designed.

This is indicative of a further set of assumptions in reviewing practice. It is not common to comment upon experimental design and method unless problems are found. This is important as one of the challenges here is that the *assumption* that method and experimental design are acceptable – even if not remarked upon positively – means that it is impossible to know whether a reviewer has truly considered these elements. The fact that such comments only come through in a negative context demonstrates the extent to which familiar patterns of behaviour are replicated – but also the degree to which PLOS's criteria must be seen as more radical. The use of structured review forms may mitigate this risk, however, and provide a way to ensure that there are comments both positive and negative on all aspects of a paper and to verify that reviewers have evaluated these aspects of a study's design.

Despite, then, PLOS's intention to modify radically the conditions under which peer review is conducted, reviewers' behaviours turn out to be far more resistant to change. When allowed to make free-form comment, reviewers revert to the practices seen elsewhere. In a context in which reviewers are working under severe time constraints, it is easier and pragmatic for them to behave in ways to which they are already accustomed. Next we speculate more on the complex drivers of institutional change and the ways in which PLOS does or does not fulfil the actual conditions necessary for radical practice to emerge.

Are Reviews in PLOS ONE *More Critically Constructive?*

The viciousness and power dynamics of peer-review feedback are often noted anecdotally and in formal studies (Belluz 2015; Berkenkotter 1995; Ceci and Peters 1982; Eve 2013; Moore et al. 2017; Shatz 1996; Silbiger and Stubler 2019), particularly when conducted under conditions of anonymity. Recent work has also shown that reviewers relay unprofessional, damaging, or even racist comments that may disproportionately affect traditionally underrepresented groups in the sciences (e.g. Silbiger and Stubler 2019). We found plenty of evidence in our tagging exercise at *PLOS ONE* to support the assertion that peer-review comments can be extremely direct (and likely emotionally bruising for authors). This included blunt appraisals but also instances where reviewers attempted to assume the career status of the authors or postulate that the work was 'salami slicing' of a PhD thesis. Statements with negative sentiment written by reviewers for the consumption of authors attached to the 'outcome' tag included the following: 'in summary, this manuscript as currently conceived and written should not be published in any reputable peer reviewed journal'; 'this paper has serious problems and needs to be completely rewritten'; '[this] manuscript is in many ways unclear and not suitable for publication'; 'these findings alone represent a minimal manuscript with effectively no major selling points to warrant publication'; 'the manuscript reads very much like a portion of a thesis rather than a self-contained manuscript for public dissemination'; 'the bulk of the writing is conjecture, speculation, unsupported theories, statements that lack data, etc.'; 'there is essentially no possibility of publication in the current format'; 'these findings are not worth much of a publication, much less a publication in PLoS'; 'the text is ridiculously unsupported, to the point where I would have been embarrassed to submit such a manuscript'; 'I could complain more and more ... but this manuscript is so poor that I am surprised it made it past editorial review'; and 'this is a poorly conceived paper with muddled logic which has no point.'

While such feedback is direct, its ire is aimed at a range of different actors within the manuscript environment. Some of these remarks attempt to deflect direct criticism of the authors themselves, commenting on the 'the manuscript', 'the text', and the 'the paper'. That is, by focusing remarks on the document, such statements can avoid personal insinuations. This is not to say that such feedback actually does this; as can be seen, personal attack and author comment are rife. Remarking, for instance, that 'I would have been embarrassed to submit such a manuscript' realigns the criticism at the author, rather than at the work. Finally, it is interesting to note the instances where criticism is directed at the editorial process and the assumptions that sit behind such assertions. The note that 'this manuscript is so poor that I am surprised it made it past editorial review' squarely places the blame for pre-filtering on the editors at *PLOS ONE*. It also assumes that the role of the first-stage editorial sweep is to ensure that reviewers' time is not wasted in the appraisal of extremely poor manuscripts. Of course, the prerequisite for this is implicit consensus between the general editor and a subject specialist about what constitutes a 'bad' manuscript. In turn, this relies upon the reviewers understanding the unique review criteria of *PLOS ONE* in the same way as the general editor. It also relies on a congruence of expectation around language and expression, which are, of course, particular to the authors' linguistic proficiency in English as well as the stylistic predilections of the home discipline of the subject specialist.

The sentiment arc of negative feedback also did not conform to our structural expectations. The secondary literature in organisational studies has, in recent years, evaluated whether the widespread practice of sugar-coated negative feedback is an effective strategy for managers (Bergen, Bressler, and Campbell 2014; Daniels 2009). We speculated that reviewers might adopt such an approach – colloquially referred to as a 'shit sandwich' – based on previous studies in the field (Fortanet 2008; Samraj 2016, 79–80). Such feedback would be described by a sentiment arc that began with positive remarks, and then moved to criticisms, before finally ending by returning to positive appraisals. This approach is designed to make it easier for reviewers to deliver hard-hitting feedback without appearing uncharitable while also recognising any positive aspects of the paper under review. It is a model of feedback desired by at least some early-career researchers who want to see 'some points for improvement' but who believe that it can 'help improve articles if the positives are also clearly highlighted' (O'Brien, Graf, and McKellar 2019, 8). However, of the fourteen papers that we tagged that scored between −7 and −10 sentiment in the 'outcome' or 'overarching comment' categories – that is, papers that were strongly rejected – not a single one received a positive sentiment of greater than +3 at any point in any other category. (For the purposes of aggregation, where a single statement received multiple tag assignations and, therefore, multiple sentiment scores, we took the mean of these scores and plotted this as a single point.)

More broadly, reviews that scored in this range for these categories generally exhibited consistently negative sentiment throughout, with the majority (nine) never scoring above the neutral zero point at all. Although the sample size here is small, from this, we conclude that at least some reviewers in *PLOS ONE* who deliver unfavourable verdicts are direct and unambiguous in their negative feedback and do not tend to 'sandwich' their statements. This is in contrast to previous studies which located instances of sandwiching practices, albeit noting that 'a good news opening is no guarantee ... of a happy ending for the author' (Belcher 2007, 10). The lack of sugar-coating of feedback may be perceived as discouraging, but from the previously cited literature in other domains, such as business management, direct and unambiguous comments, even if negative, are more useful in delivering clear, actionable, and interpretable reports that are less subject to miscomprehension (such ambiguity in reports was a key finding of Bakanic, McPhail, and Simon 1989).

That said, some commonalities in sentiment arc appear among the very most negative reviews that we tagged, but these are potentially occurring by chance since they are few in number. Specifically, reviews that scored a -10 in the 'outcome' or 'overarching comment' category tended to show a decline in sentiment approximately one-third of the way through the review, with an upwards spike at the two-thirds point, as seen in Figure 3.

By contrast, the strongly positive reports that we tagged – those that yielded a score of between $+7$ and $+10$ for 'outcome' or 'overarching comment' – tended to exhibit much wider variance in their sentiment markers. There was also a greater commonality in their sentiment arcs, as shown in Figure 4.

All of the strongly positive reports that we tagged began with glowing praise and their most positive remarks before falling down the sentiment scale. Indeed, it is the reports that recommend a positive outcome (including requests for minor revisions) that appear most likely to exhibit the shit-sandwich formulation, although this turns out to be misleading. The sandwich shape is actually due to the fact that extremely positive sentiment scores for 'outcome' and 'overarching comment' are almost always comments on the fact that revisions have been addressed, before going into more minor quibbles, and then encountering the rest of the original, more critical review. For instance, most of these reports begin by remarking favourably upon the revisions that have been undertaken on the manuscripts: 'The authors have addressed the review comments I made completely and effectively and I look forward to seeing the completed manuscript

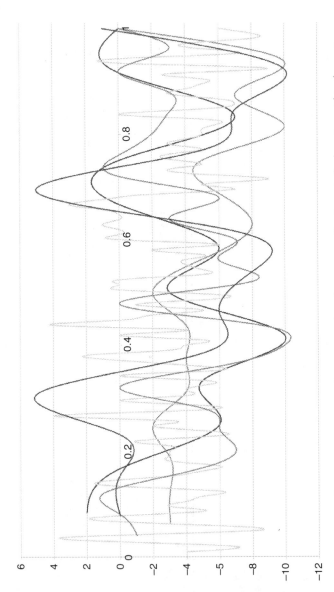

Figure 3 Extremely negative review sentiment arcs, plotted on a normalised x-axis for location within the review document against sentiment on the y-axis. Each line represents a report.

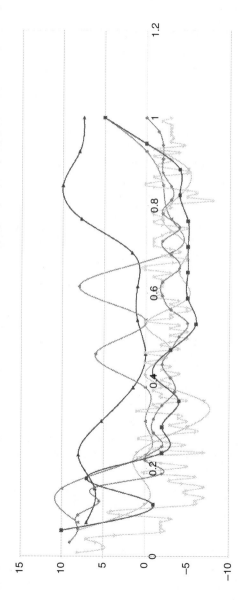

Figure 4 Extremely positive review sentiment arcs, plotted on a normalised x-axis for location within the review document against sentiment on the y-axis. Each line represents a report.

in press'; 'The authors have successfully address all the comments highlighted in the previous review of the manuscript'; 'This manuscript is significantly improved over the previous version'; 'The authors have made revisions and answered all the questions the review raised'; and 'The authors have adequately addressed the comments raised in a previous round of review and I think this manuscript is now acceptable for publication.' Indeed, we only encountered one report that scored highly positive for 'outcome' and 'overarching comment' sentiment that was not a statement about revision: 'I don't have anything to add or suggest to this manuscript and for the first time, I will accept this paper just as it is.' Although again deduced from a low sample size, this suggests that almost all highly positive outcomes are the result of a revisions process and that first-round acceptance at *PLOS ONE* is a rare occurrence. In contrast to the most negative reports that we examined, these reviews, although positive, straddled the neutral line and contained many more critical comments.

If PLOS's criteria aimed to create a more constructive review environment – one in which comments were more objective and less *ad hominem* – then it is not clear that it has yet succeeded. Reviewers appear to be as blunt and direct as in any other title. Comments are frequently bruising but do at least, as a result, avoid interpretational ambiguity.

How Much of a Role Does the Authors' Language Play in Reviewers' Verdicts?

Many reviews focused their critique upon expression (that is, the way a paper was written). This varied hugely by reviewer, but one review that we evaluated contained 106 separate line-by-line recommendations for often minor or trivial adjustments of expression. This level of detail was certainly rare; in this case, it was often a combination of typo errors ('smaple should be sample') and clarifications of expression ('I wasn't sure what the authors meant by X'). Clearly, though, it is also a mistake to regard the scholarly communications workflow as a steady, linear progression from peer review (encompassing a 'pure' intellectual and objective appraisal of the work), through copyediting (language changes), into typesetting (producing galleys), before proofing (a final check that no further errors have been introduced), and publication.

Instead, peer review often seems to cross over with copyediting, in particular. As *PLOS ONE* does not perform copyediting, this is actually, also, an element on which reviewers are specifically invited to comment. Sixty per cent (47) of the reports that we studied made some comment on expression or pointed out typos in the manuscript under review. While some disciplines, such as history, have argued that the form of expression in their field is more central to their intellectual concerns (Mandler 2013, 556), the natural sciences, exemplified here in *PLOS ONE*, also take expression extremely seriously. On the one hand, this is at least in part because imprecision of language can lead to misunderstanding of the underlying scientific facts that a paper intends to communicate. Indeed, linguistics and language cannot wholly be separated from the intellectual content of a paper. As one reviewer remarked, with their own expressive errors in the sentence: 'nonthless [*sic*] the article is not well write [*sic*], with many ambiguous sentence's and interpretations, that makes difficult the under-standing.' While this type of statement can appear careless and hypocritical, it could be that this reviewer is a non-native English speaker as it is widely acknowledged that it is easier to read second languages than to produce new and correct statements in them, but we do not presume this here.

On the other hand, though, often the language 'errors' that are corrected by peer reviewers go far further than would be necessary merely to under-stand the work and veer into the realm of preference: 'Also be careful about split infinitives: "experimentally shown" is grammatically incorrect even though it is used in casual English' (although in this case the example given could only be a borderline instance of a split complement, unless 'shown' is a typo for 'show'). In any case, this reviewer continues: "You 'show experimentally' much the same that you do not 'boldly go' rather than 'go boldly.'" The specific reference to *Star Trek* in 'boldly go' is also culturally contingent. This type of pedantic (although not necessarily unhelpful) cor-rection by a type of reviewer that we call 'peer copyeditors' extends all the way down to the placement of commas: 'represented, whereas is an incorrect use of a comma'. Further the advice given in this space of language editing appears often to be less thorough than in other areas. On some occasions in our corpus, native English speakers believe that simply drawing attention to an inaccuracy of language – without any supporting statements – is sufficient to make an error apparent. This is not always true, though. For instance, one comment simply read: 'Line 130: Piece-by-piece' and it was not clear to us precisely what error was being highlighted.

The detection of language errors in peer-review reports was also used to police the tone of manuscripts, ensuring that the scientific record remains one couched in a formal level of written discourse: 'Line 305: the inclusion of a suspension point [ellipsis] in the text is too casual for a main body of text within a peer-reviewed manuscript.' Certainly, this speaks to the fact that peer review is a process that sees itself as protecting the public perception of science, and the ways in which language registers may confer reputational advantage or damage. Much in the same way that radio presenters in the United Kingdom were once expected to speak only with received pronunciation, in ensuring presentational care over manuscripts, peer reviewers often consider the challenging matter of public, or even just intra-scientific, presentation (Sangster 2008; Trudgill 2000, 7). This comes with the advantage of not only ensuring that papers use the 'correct' linguistic expression for their object of study and are, as a result, accurate (while also maintaining an acceptability and appropriateness of register) but also ensuring that the language of science has a formal mimetic quality. There seems to be an underlying concern that if the language of and expression within a paper is sloppy, the team could also have been careless in their scientific practice. Judgements over the use of English language are thus made or used supposedly to reflect the quality of science and thought beneath a paper.

As we noted in Chapter One, though, this can be problematic. It is perfectly possible to construct and conduct a sound scientific experiment without being a fluent writer or speaker of English. The prevalence of comment on expression suggests, though, that peer reviewers in *PLOS ONE* regard the communication of scientific research as part of the research process itself. Expressive language is both deemed within the evaluative remit of reviewers and seen as integrally entwined both with the reputation of scientific discourse (and its seriousness) and with a mimetic quality that must somehow reflect the accuracy of the underpinning science. Given that modes of expression are preferential and rooted within the pragmatic language community of the reader, this puts some strain on the argument that PLOS's review criteria result in a process that is designed to efface subjectivity.

How Much of Reviewer Behaviour Can Be Controlled/ Anticipated?

The recent literature around peer review has suggested many ways in which policies and procedures might improve our practices (Allen et al. 2019). Many of the reports contained sentences that requested additional information that was expected, but not found, in the manuscript. In our taxonomy, the tags 'elaboration' and 'omission' are emblematic of this phenomenon in which an absence is detected within the paper and additional information is requested. This is different, in some cases, from a missing ethics section, for instance, and can pertain more to an imprecision in the language used within a manuscript. For example, one reviewer asked 'what was the nature of the protein samples?' while another specified that 'it would be better to add a table listing the main methods published in the literature.'

In these cases, there is an obvious question: How do reviewers come to any conclusion about what is missing or what should be present? Sometimes this is based on subject knowledge. As noted, a subject specialist wanted to know more detail on the particular nature of protein samples under discussion, presumably because specific types of proteins might have behaved differently under the experimental conditions. Another example of this in our tagged corpus was the statement that 'in the absence of this information, it is difficult to ascertain whether [this genetic marker] is an independent prognostic factor in the [condition under discussion].' Such omission in this case is related to interpretation and method. The requested addition to the manuscript in this instance would allow the reader to link clearly the outcome in the patient group to a single expressive genetic marker. However, this could be seen as much as a critique of method as a simple statement on omission depending on whether the absent information is actually available. In other words: if the manuscript author(s) is (are) unable to provide the missing information, because it is unknown and unaccounted for in their experiment, then this is a failure of *method*. If the information is available, but has simply been omitted from the manuscript, then this is simply an issue of presentation of necessary context in the document. Other instances of this method/presentation ambiguity in omission statements abound. For instance: 'for example, [redacted] status is known in only a few patients, [genetic] mutation status is not reported and cytogenetics/molecular cytogenetic classification is missing' and 'important information are [*sic*] missing preventing the comprehension of the results.'

On the other hand, the earlier second example – on listing the methods in a table – is a presentational comment as much as an omission. Certainly, it recommends the insertion of an artefact that was not present in the manuscript at the time of review. However, this is not linked, as in the previous cases, to any matter of interpretation or method but rather to the clarity of expression of the manuscript. Such matters are preferential to each reviewer but may also be linked to expectations of presentational norms within disciplinary sub-communities. In smaller, more niche journals, such presentational styles might be explicitly specified: 'a summary of relevant methods from the secondary literature should be presented in a tabular form', for example. However, in larger 'mega-journals' such as *PLOS ONE*, it is far more difficult to police intra-disciplinary norms except through tacit reviewer expectations that are rarely made explicit. Junior scholars who consult the journal and read previous articles for presentational context may be confused by variance of styles within a single venue, as they will be unable to spot coherence between spaces (because it does not exist).

Omission and requests for elaboration were clearly linked in our taxonomy and usually these tags occurred together. This indicates that in most cases there is overlap between omissions and hermeneutic contexts that can be clarified by additional explanation. Statements tagged purely with 'omission' or those in conjunction with 'presentation' were usually more of the presentational (and perhaps superficial) nature described earlier. In this way, it is often the case that multidimensional appraisals of intersecting labels/tags can give a better context for understanding the function of a specific statement.

In these instances of absence, we suggest that it may be worthwhile for journals to think about explicit matters that require consideration. Just as a conflict of interest statement is overtly required and requested of reviewers, a clear delineation of elements that should be present in a manuscript could help to foster reviewing practice with greater homogeneity of requests for additional information. Such comments on omission, though, also draw attention to the unspoken assumptions made by reviewers. They are remarks upon *expectation*, which can only be drawn by those familiar with an outside environment. For venues that wish to change cultures of review, this presents some severe difficulties in anticipating what reviewers will want to see, but that new criteria may rule out. How does one account for the Rumsfeldian 'unknown unknowns' under such a paradigm?

To What Extent Do Reviewers Understand New Paradigms of Review?

To close this chapter, we want briefly to comment on the occasional references that we found that pertain to processes of scholarly communications within peer-review reports. We have already noted that occasionally reviewers remark on the unique novelty criteria of *PLOS ONE*. However, very occasionally reviewers refer to more unusual practices in a type of scientific meta-commentary.

A good example of this is a remark on grey literature that we encountered, in which a reviewer wrote: 'I consider it acceptable to take key results from grey literature and to submit the material for peer review and publication in an archival journal.' 'Grey literature' refers to material that is publicly or internally available but has not been published in conventional academic channels (Adams et al. 2016; Saleh, Ratajeski, and Bertolet 2014). It can refer to blog posts, internal corporate reports, pamphlets, and other forms. Of interest in this particular statement is that the reviewer expresses an opinion on the acceptability of submitting such material as reference sources within peer-reviewed venues. However, it is notable that the reviewer then goes on to state that if such practices are conducted, the paper itself must be of an extremely high quality and of significance. That is, in this reviewer's view, only papers of the highest quality and significance should be permitted to cite grey literature.

Similarly, there were comments on the functioning of referencing and how such systems should serve within scholarly communication environments. For instance, one reviewer remarked that 'this reference is advertising, not science.' Such a statement relies on an understanding of the functions of both referencing and citation – a complex subject that varies from discipline to discipline (with a diverse set of motivations underpinning the reasons why people make reference to or cite work) (Cronin 1984, 1998, 2000; Erikson and Erlandson 2014) – and a definition of science that is not immediately clear from the context of this sentence. It is possible that the reviewer believes that there is a conflict of interest here and that the citation is being used merely to inflate the citation counts of the author. Alternatively, the phrase 'advertising not science' has found a prominent place in various open science movements that promote the sharing of data. Indeed, Graham Steel has remarked that 'publishing research without data is simply advertising, not science', the implication being that without the means to verify the underlying study, most scientific content is worthless (Steel 2013).[3]

It is not possible, in this second instance, to determine which of these possibilities is under consideration, but such comments nonetheless open a fascinating window into the ways in which reviewers can begin to challenge established scientific practices through their comments. We did not specifically tag these statements with any kind of 'meta' label, but we would suggest that future studies – or work at publishing houses – consider the ways in which reviewers may, cumulatively and over time, exert pressures on the usual norms of reviewing practices through such meta-scientific statements about scholarly communications. In this way, it may become feasible to chart the extent to which institutional diktats of change are enacted on the ground. It should become possible, over time, to see the changing expectations of reviewers' cultural practice embedded in their implicit demands of manuscripts and what they deem to be missing, thus giving a benchmark as to the permeation of new cultures of review.

Commonalities between Reviews

In our tagging exercise, we were only able to explore a very small proportion of the review database. Indeed, the effort involved in team-tagging the

---

[3] Comments along these lines have a long history, seemingly originating in Buckheit and Donoho's (1995) 'Wavelab and Reproducibility Research' which comments on arguments of Jon Claerbout and offers to 'distill Claerbout's insight into a slogan' in the following form: 'An article about computational science in a scientific publication is not the scholarship itself, it is merely advertising of the scholarship.'

reports was substantial. The process involved detailed negotiations between team members and a triplicate replication of labour in each case. Recent developments in natural language processing, however, have led to various practices of 'distant' or 'machine' reading (see Da 2019; Eve 2019; Moretti 2013, 2007; Piper 2018; Underwood 2017, 2019).

We wondered whether it might be possible, thinking within such paradigms, to train a predictive model that was able to identify and to tag accurately peer-review statements, thereby allowing us to extrapolate our quantitative findings across the entire *PLOS ONE* review corpus. To conduct this test, we built a multi-class and multi-label text classifier based on the TenCent NeuralClassifier toolkit (*An Open-Source Neural Hierarchical Multi-Label Text Classification Toolkit: Tencent/NeuralNLP-NeuralClassifier* 2019).

Although multi-class and multi-label text classification is a difficult task and even though we were only possessed of a relatively minimal, albeit robust, training set, the neural network was good at classifying certain types of input text. In particular, the network performed well at recognising requests for revision and/or outcome statements. For example, the generic statement 'I do not recommend publication' was tagged by the network as pertaining to 'revision' and 'outcome'. Some other types of broad statements were also accurately classified: 'In particular I am left confused as to how the results fit in here' was marked as 'ambiguity' and 'cohesion' by the software.

However, the specific challenges of implementing an accurate classification system were many. First, the tagged data proved insufficient for these purposes. The labour-intensive processes of triplicate tagging gave us the confidence that we needed in the material that had been tagged, but this came at the expense of volume. Further, since each tagged statement was relatively short, it was difficult to train natural-language processing toolkits to identify salient features; there is not a huge volume in each case for the network to identify. As noted, there are also instances where we did not find and tag particular types of statements, such as those pertaining to ethics. Finally, since each statement was written by a different author (reviewer), with different primary languages, the strength of these linguistic differentiations – as opposed to the words used within different types of classificatory statements – appears to be pulled to the fore (for more on authorship signals against others, see Allison et al. 2011; Jockers 2013). As such, this study is limited to a relatively small sample size with a relatively good accuracy level within that sample.

Hence, while the network appears to work well at classifying statements that have appeared in almost all reviews – for instance, the outcome example given – it performed poorly at identifying less frequent types, such as 'fallibility'. The network was unable, for example, to ascribe a label to the statement 'I must confess that I am not an expert with respect to these methods', a clear assertion of fallibility. Further, various statements around originality were not tagged with any accuracy. For instance, 'There is nothing technically wrong with the paper, but it is not that original' was marked as an 'overarching comment', which is a fair assessment. However, no label noting that this was a statement about originality or novelty was ascribed, regardless of the training parameters that we fed to the network.

In short, while our experiment in using machine learning to examine the entire corpus of reviews might have worked well for certain types of statements, such as those pertaining to outcome, the uncertainty around and low levels of accuracy mean that any quantitative analysis based on the broader corpus, read at distance, would be unacceptably imprecise. Nonetheless, the moments of success in the network seem to indicate that those with broader resources for tagging and access to a large corpus of review reports might, in future, see some benefit in using this approach. For instance, we can envisage situations where such a network could detect hostile tone and warn the reviewer that they are being overly harsh or *ad hominem*. We could also imagine situations in which such a classifier could distinguish reviews that were structured in an unusual/idiosyncratic manner. While this would not rule out the review from being useful, it could give an indication that the reviewer is inexperienced or working away from norms of the form. That said, if publishers used the network to insist on normative practices in review, then this could stifle new ways of writing and operating.

A further method for distant reading the corpus is, of course, to conduct a simple text search through the reviews. This is how we identified the 'missing' statements on ethics to which we earlier referred. This can be useful to find examples of specific kinds of practice. For instance, to identify overly aggressive reports we used a simple tool, 'grep' (globally search a regular expression and print), to look for instances of the word 'useless' in the top-800 longest reports. This yielded harsh reports that included phrases such as 'Fig 12 is almost useless'; 'the null model seems somewhat useless'; 'remove the repeated useless sentences'; 'I found the [secondary subject matter] results to be EXTREMELY distracting, and essentially useless'; 'this work appears to be all but useless' and so on. What such searching cannot tell us, though, is the prevalence of such practices. For instance, the previous examples were found using an extremely simple keyword search pulled from the top of our heads. There will be many instances of *ad hominem* or vicious attacks that use different terms and the only reliable way, at present, to identify these is to read and to tag the reports themselves.

In addition to this, capital letters (such as 'EXTREMELY' in the given example) are relatively easy to detect and sometimes indicate strong sentiment of one kind or another. However, detection of these is not as simple as a regular expression ('\b[A-Z][A-Z]+\b') as this will also pull out the many acronyms used in scientific practice ('BDNF', 'ROC', etc.). It is also not clear that capital letters denote strong sentiment in one direction or another; 'WOW' can indicate 'WOW this is a brilliant paper', but it can equally likely specify 'WOW, this paper was terrible.' Furthermore, on occasion, capital letters are used to denote section headings and/or specific portions of a paper ('in the METHOD section'). In this way, the extraction of capital letters – without a pre-built blacklist of words to exclude – is likely to result in many false positives.

Another way of exploring the corpus at scale is to use the techniques of topic modelling. Topic modelling generally uses a process called 'latent Dirichlet allocation' (LDA) to cluster terms that probabilistically co-occur in similar contexts. This is a useful way to explore a dataset and to infer the groups of terms that most frequently crop up together, that is, which 'topics' are explored within a corpus ('a three-level hierarchical Bayesian model, in which each item of a collection is modeled as a finite mixture over an underlying set of topics') (Blei, Ng, and Jordan 2003, 993). As Ben Schmidt notes, this approach 'does a good job giving an overview of the contents of large textual collections; it can provide some intriguing new artifacts to study; and it even holds . . . some promise for structuring non-lexical data like geographic points' (2012).

However, LDA is also a dangerous method: there is no way to infer *why* topics have been grouped together. In particular, surprising groupings that appear to exhibit coherence may not be as well bound as we would like to think. As Schmidt continues:

> [S]till, excitement about the use of topic models for discovery needs to be tempered with skepticism about how often the unexpected juxtapositions LDA creates will be helpful, and how often merely surprising. A poorly supervised machine learning algorithm is like a bad research assistant. It might produce some unexpected constellations that show flickers of deeper truths; but it will also produce tedious, inexplicable, or misleading results. (2012)

That said, as an exploratory exercise that others may wish to take further, we produced a twenty-topic model using the MALLET tool based on the same corpus of 800 reports using the default hyperparameters and with stop words excluded. The results for this are shown in Table 2.

Some of these topics appear easy to interpret. Group one, composed of 'authors', 'manuscript', and 'paper' and so on cluster meta-statements about the paper, its submission, the review process. It is curious, though, that 'important' should find its way into the work here (although 'not important' would also trigger this, so no sentiment value should be inferred). Certainly, the word 'important' can appear in multiple contexts. For instance, 'it is important that the author address these points' is as likely a statement as 'this paper is extremely important.' Nonetheless, given that *PLOS ONE* specifically disavows 'importance' from its criteria, it is significant that the term should appear so prominently among statements that are otherwise common in opening gambits.

Topic four, by contrast, clearly pertains to the mechanics of a paper and suggested corrections. Its functional emphasis on the 'line', 'sentence', 'page', 'figure', 'table', and so forth – coupled with 'suggest', 'add', 'replace', and 'delete' – is the archetypical set of terms that we find in revision requests. In

Table 2 A topic model of the 800 longest reports in our database of reviews
at *PLOS ONE*

Topic Number	Topic Terms
1	authors manuscript paper study comments data review results current previous discussion work addressed major provide reviewer research information important studies
2	interests competing samples genetic dna populations population gene pcr table strains sequences figure structure loci sequencing individuals analysis chromosomes number
3	paper data case make point time clear important find fact understand general evidence e.g. i.e. model number high approach literature
4	line lines page sentence paragraph change suggest section figure results text table discussion reference manuscript remove delete add replace information
5	genes gene expression analysis number sequences sequence genome rna authors expressed species biological fig methods transcripts data results transcriptome proteins
6	model method models paper approach parameters system distribution set network number dataset parameter distributions author proposed performance simulations equation networks
7	species study habitat lines area model spatial population areas line fish variables sites models distance size individuals data prey year
8	study treatment patients group participants trial intervention studies outcome pain analysis groups clinical outcomes research control care reported patient measures
9	patients study blood clinical studies disease plasma levels authors activity acute group tissue serum negative ace sensitivity mir cortisol healthy

Table 2 Cont.

Topic Number	Topic Terms
10	social behavior females males male authors individuals scer_scrt lcl study female group behaviors human sex calls behaviour pointing sexual attention
11	fire area page e.g. subject trees specific stand bone signals motion intensity study science frequency subjects biochemistry atmospheric stands fires
12	food hsv animals infection mice diet authors bees response dose resistance treatment weight pigs bacteria immune intake group larvae virus
13	participants task authors condition experiment effect stimuli results memory performance responses effects experiments stimulation response conditions experimental visual trials learning
14	cells authors cell figure fig expression data shown protein experiments levels control show mrna mice state manuscript results effect antibody
15	species phylogenetic taxa tree xxx based diversity sequences analysis clade character genus specimens support trees present phylogeny group taxonomic found
16	age health risk table page women population study prevalence model factors children results years variables cases analysis paragraph hiv year
17	null partly disease n/a cancer vaccine hpv page cervical women vaccination safety doi group gardasil adverse rate don't map human
19	data results authors analysis table methods study differences significant discussion statistical figure time section values effect test information sample size

Table 2 Cont.

Topic Number	Topic Terms
19	species water soil temperature change growth plant plants concentrations climate samples concentration biomass sites fish site study conditions carbon community
20	fig protein binding manuscript light proteins figure structure shown images domain mutant site sequence image residues cry region structures pax

our experience of tagging, such language is prevalent during line-by-line commentaries that usually take the form of 'line 123: suggest adding X'.

Several of the topics relate to subject matter that is clearly of disciplinary interest to and prominent within *PLOS ONE*. Topics two and five, for instance, are concerned with genetics. Topic seven appears to be biology; topics eight and nine circle around medicine and clinical trials; topic ten relates to reproduction, mating, and sexuality; topic twelve seems to indicate dietary behaviours; topic fifteen is about biological taxonomies; topic sixteen is on ageing.

Of course, anyone who knows anything about *PLOS ONE* might have guessed that such terms would cluster and be found as separate strata. For us, the more useful indicators are not the subject groupings, which one would expect, but the functional parameters. We can anticipate scenarios under which knowledge of the distinct linguistic layer of line-by-line corrections, for instance, could be extracted and formed into editorial 'to-do' lists. We could also imagine automatic detection of appraisal of novelty and importance and a flagging system that could warn the editor of such an approach (and that it should not be used in the judgement of articles). The challenge, as ever with topic modelling, is that the topics that seem clearly thematically clustered are obvious, while the ones that exhibit less coherence (say, topic twenty) are baffling.

4 PLOS, Institutional Change, and the Future of Peer Review

How Successful Was PLOS in Changing Peer Review?

While this book has focused specifically on the analysis of peer review, its histories, and its futures, the implications in reality are far wider. We have actually been speaking about broader institutional change and its drivers. A key point on such institutional change was voiced by Harold Varmus, one of the original proponents of PLOS, who, when asked what he might have done differently, noted 'just how much effort it takes to convince the scientific community to make a change in their publication practices' (Poynder 2006a). Yet PLOS set out to change the way that review was conducted. It saw the flaws in the existing system and aimed to create a better structure, a utopianism in the non-pejorative sense of the word. How successful, though, was PLOS in changing the world?

One of the most notable impacts of PLOS's practice has been the proliferation of new venues adopting novel peer-review mechanisms. For instance, as noted earlier, the F1000 platforms that power systems such as Wellcome Open Research run on post-publication mechanisms. PLOS's early radicalism paved the road for these types of platforms in ways that would not have otherwise been possible. Further, although we argue that PLOS's impact must be evaluated in distributed terms across the heterogeneous set of new organisations that it has spawned, *PLOS ONE* itself continues to receive a high volume of annual submissions, indicating a demand for its systems of peer review that facilitate rapid publication of results that do not necessarily claim to be earth shattering.

However, in terms of reviewer behaviour, our work shows that PLOS's readers have not wholly gotten the message of change. For instance, one of the core goals of the new PLOS review model was to change appraisal from novelty and significance to technical soundness, reproducibility, and scientific accuracy. Yet it is clear from our analysis that reviewers still frequently mention novelty and significance (albeit not always as a discriminator for publication and with the caveats set out earlier in the section on topic modelling) but that they rarely remark upon reproducibility. In other words: changing the criteria of peer review to ask reviewers to appraise aspects of science different from those with which they are familiar appears a necessary but insufficient condition of change. The norms of gatekeeping creep back in, despite such changes.

Reviewer civility is a harder aspect to appraise. Certainly, one of the extant criticisms of the peer-review system is that it is aggressive, oppressive, and *ad hominem*. Reviews in *PLOS ONE* continue to exhibit remarkable directness and use language that is likely to be upsetting to authors. However, whether this is bad practice is unclear. In cutting to the chase, such reviews provide unambiguous feedback as to the acceptability or otherwise of the manuscript. Hence, it may be that strong, direct statements avoid future disappointment for authors who might misinterpret sandwiched or hedged reports. That said, judgements based on language can be prejudicial to non-native English speakers, which can extend outwards into a coloniality of gatekeeping (Eve and Gray 2020). Balancing the need for accurate expression against merely preferential considerations, in an environment where there is no round of professional copyediting, can prove difficult.

Why, though, do such instances of policy change not translate into real-world action? In some ways, this is a collective action problem. The unspoken but shared belief among reviewers that they should act according to broader community norms, rather than the 'outsider' logic of a single venue, could partly account for this. Such external pressures are even clearer in the case of new journals that wish to get off the ground but, at the same time, alter social systems. This is because journals are, to some degree, knowledge clubs (Buchanan 1965; Hartley 2015; Potts et al. 2017; Sandler and Tschirhart 1980). A club is, in the classic definition, 'a voluntary group deriving mutual benefits from sharing one or more of the following: production costs, the members' characteristics, or a good characterized by excludable benefits' (Sandler and Tschirhart 1997, 335). The binding commonalities of the intellectual communities that use academic publishing systems make club theory a compelling way to describe such structures.

If we accept the assertion that a journal is a club, a different question arises: Is/was *PLOS ONE* even a journal? As Hartley et al. note, '[a]t launch, *PLOS ONE* had no community beyond enthusiastic supporters of its publishing organization' (2019, 31). Its brand – the excludable benefit – that it offered to authors was radicalism. Within academia, this is a very small club indeed. Certainly, other members' characteristics were not shared by the broader population of the academy. Academics schooled in conventional models of peer review and who believe(d) in the filtering mechanisms of peer review as a valid way to reduce reading load did not share characteristics with the radicals who supported *PLOS ONE*. The very idea of diluting scarcity by publishing replication studies and anything that was technically sound also abolished any shared competitive quest for prestige, the excludable benefit of publication in many titles. *PLOS ONE* also failed to bind academics by discipline. Again, as Hartley et al. put it, 'the quality assurance associated with the prestige good is no longer efficiently provided by an informed knowledge club. A journal covering sociology and neuroscience invokes a community that is too broad, diffuse, and uncertain to ensure that quality assurance is consistent' (2019, 32). Add to this that many academics were – and still are – opposed to open access and one has the perfect storm. Given that the radicals who valued *PLOS ONE* at the start were opposed to many of the characteristics that apply to most journals, it is almost the case that they had created the venue as a club whose membership could be described by Groucho Marx's famous quip: 'I don't want to belong to any club that would accept me as one of its members.'

In short, perhaps the reason that *PLOS ONE*'s edicts on peer reviewers' behaviours seem to have had less effect than one might believe (or hope depending on one's inclinations) is that it tried to hit so many moving targets at once. By demolishing disciplinarity, peer review for significance and novelty, copyediting, print publication, and paywalls – all at the same time – *PLOS ONE* almost destroyed any binding notion of community that might have survived. Perhaps a better question is the following: How has PLOS's vision had so much of an impact on the world, given the short-comings of its community model?

Several answers present themselves. First, the club model for under-standing journals has limitations. Other kinds of goods and clubs are in play beyond those tied directly to scholarly communities that are capable of providing sufficient benefits to be sustained. Journals like *Nature* do not serve a specific identifiable community with common scholarly norms and practices. Rather, they create a 'social network market' where the club good is the prestige of being in a selective group of authors. It is possible that *PLOS ONE* did in fact provide a similar kind of community, albeit at a lower level of prestige, based on a recognised brand that signifies sufficient publication to be of value. This would mean that recognisable scholarly communities do not matter as much to the lifecycle of journals as Hartley et al. (2019) want to claim. It is likely that the simple club theoretic model is an incomplete way of thinking about journals.

A second possibility is that PLOS came along at the right time and that there was more of a radical community lurking than suspected. In this case, *PLOS ONE* served a pent-up demand. This is an interesting assertion with respect to group dynamics, as the BMC Series of journals could be argued to have had a similar if less explicit model within a more traditional set of separate journals. If *PLOS ONE* was serving a nascent community with pent-up demand, that community must have been spread too thinly within the disciplines that the BMC Series was serving separately; therefore, the cross-disciplinary nature was actually an advantage. Of course, it is also possible that the BMC Series laid the groundwork that made *PLOS ONE* seem less radical to certain communities, which in turn may have also encouraged engagement from latent radicals, willing to emerge once the concept had proven itself.

Third, shifting funder attitudes at the governmental, philanthropic, and institutional levels adopted similar rhetorics to PLOS and, as such, changed the desirable club membership criteria among academics. It could be that by having a good idea and getting it in front of the people with the money, PLOS created a community using soft power. Another way of putting this is that PLOS was made safe as its radicalisms around peer review, disciplinarity, process, and open access became normalised within institutions. That said, however one spins it at the broader level of authorship, we also have clear evidence from our work that reviewers have *not* internalised such radicalism. PLOS may have won over the bodies of its authors as a new community, but their souls seem to remain firmly in extant camps.

There is also the possibility that our expectations around timescales are poorly calibrated here. Several figures in recent years have lamented the 'slow' pace of change (Cockerill 2014; Poynder 2017, 2019), marking almost twenty years since the signing of the three initial declarations on open access (Chan et al. 2002; 'Berlin Declaration on Open Access to Knowledge in the Sciences and Humanities', 2003; Suber et al. 2003). A comparison with the timescale for the original uptake of peer review is both enlightening and frustrating. As Aileen Fyfe notes, '[t]he practice that we now recognise as "peer review" (but not the term itself) emerged in the early 19th century.' It was not until the 1830s that the systemic use of peer review came to the fore – almost two hundred years after the establishment of the *Philosophical Transactions* journal – even if '[t]hereafter, refereeing quickly became a normal part of the publication process at the learned societies' (Fyfe 2015; see also Moxham and Fyfe 2018).

The original development of 'peer review', then, went through a series of evolutionary changes. However, more important to note is that, at the time of the emergence of refereeing, the academic world was much smaller. It was not the globalised system of hyperconnected interchange that it is today, and fewer papers were published per year than there are now sometimes authors on a single paper. This created a systemic flexibility that does not exist in our time. Consensus building for change between 200 people is easier than among 200,000; when the number of journals was extremely limited, executive editorial decisions about process would have widespread, near-total system-wide effects.

This is not the case in the current environment. A disaggregated system of publishing in which thousands of journal titles are spread among hundreds of corporate entities with differing mission goals means that interventions are always partial. Singular interventions must normally be considered as either attempts at consensus-building or as disruptions (Christensen 1997). PLOS, clearly, aimed at the latter and certainly succeeded in showing an alternative that is now cascading through the echelons of new publication venues. An example of a consensus-building approach might be seen in an organisation such as Crossref, which is composed of a member board of publishers and acts as an intermediate and governed third party to implement new metadata deposit and preservation infrastructures.

There is also the idea, however, of 'scaling small' (Adema 2018). In such efforts, the idea of systemic centralised change is abandoned in favour of accepting limited capacity but with the potential for – albeit no expectation of – horizontal spread, a kind of archipelago of radical practice. Examples of such small-scale rethinkings, radical reworkings, or demonstrations of practice can be found in groups such as the ScholarLed collective, and in entities such as punctum books, Goldsmiths Press, Open Book Publishers, Open Humanities Press, the Open Library of Humanities, and others. Usually not driven by top-down imperatives, although sometimes attracting grant funding from private and government sources, such initiatives create alternative spaces of publishing possibility, perhaps at more manageable scales than the transformative attempts of *PLOS ONE*.

Our study presented in this book has also charted some of the technical, privacy, and labour implications that we faced in our attempt to understand better the peer-review corpus at *PLOS ONE*. However, we have only really been able to scratch the surface. The time resources we expended in triplicate tagging our subset of the review corpus were substantial; yet, even with this investment, we were unable to obtain a large enough sample size/training set for machine-learning approaches to classify the corpus at scale. This resource problem also comes with some worrying future consequences. Many large multinational publishing companies have substantial access to peer-review reports from the portfolios of thousands of journals. With yearly revenues in the billions of dollars, their resources far exceed those that universities can afford. This means that if we are not careful, the people who will know the most about the peer-review processes in the academy will be corporate entities that do not necessarily share the values that we prize (see Fitzpatrick 2019 for a good articulation of the direction in which universities should consider heading; see also Montgomery et al. 2018). Given the ever-increasing metrification of evaluation processes and the conversion of large publishers to full-stack data-controlling entities, providing evaluative dashboards to university managers, this is a potentially damaging situation. We must take care to ensure that research into peer review is not *market* or *private-corporate* research, but research conducted for its own sake, in the open.

All is not lost, though. Even while portions of this book have expressed scepticism at peer review's predictive powers, we have managed both to confirm the findings of some existing studies and to refute some others. We have also been privileged to be the first group to work with *PLOS ONE*'s corpus of reviews, which differs substantially from other corpora in its criterion of 'technical soundness'. This differentiation made it possible for us to appraise the extent to which organisational change can be driven by changes to policy and guidelines. Academia may or may not advance one funeral at a time, but peer review is certainly slower to change than publisher policies in the digital age.

It is difficult, at our time of writing, to predict what peer review will look like in a decade's time. That Einstein in 1936 was surprised by a review of his work shows us the speed at which practices *can* change, and we exist today in a period in which digital accelerationism is nearly omnipresent. While we should not succumb to technological determinism, we also should not underestimate the power of new digital capabilities to create feedback loops that alter behavioural expectations. Technology can drive social change as much as social change can alter technology. Indeed, as Janis Jefferies and Sarah Kember put it, '[w]e might point to a consensual technological determinism that both undermines and structures the opposition between a culture that is free (and freely shared) and one that is, necessarily, proprietorial' (2019, 3). At the same time, it is important to note the extent to which academia has *naturalised* the story of peer review, transforming it into a supposedly timeless phenomenon, when really it is not as old as might be suspected.

Perhaps, though, one of the key takeaway points with which we wish to leave the reader is the question of digital abundance, scarcity, and the problematic powers of filtering and discovery. *PLOS ONE* is premised on the notion that in the age of the Internet, the scarcity of academic publication through high levels of filtering selection based on novelty or significance is a *false scarcity*. To some extent, this is true. There are not the constraints of page space and budget in the digital age. But there is still a cost to publishing per paper and PLOS charges to cover it. While high rejection rates based on an artificial scarcity have been blamed for exorbitant publisher costs, one could equally say the same of high-output volume publications such as *PLOS ONE*, in which universities will pay *because* something has *passed* review, rather than paying a higher cost in a subscription ecosystem for material not to appear in exclusive venues, as was the case under exclusive review criteria. The low levels of filtering also have a human cost. How we can deal with ever-rising levels of published material, even within small sub-disciplines, remains unresolved. More is published every day than can ever be read by a single person in a lifetime. This is not to say that exclusive peer review is the solution to such a problem: if we are no good at selecting *what* to publish, then there is no point claiming that this saves people time. What is clear is that value signals, communicated through various forms of peer review, will become ever more important over time – alongside machine learning and classification approaches – in directing where we spend our attention. A combined value attribution through machine curation and human sentiment seems to be the future direction of travel.

In all, though, we hope that this study will be of interest in informing future discussion on peer review but also on future change in the academy. PLOS developed a groundbreaking new paradigm that, over the course of a decade and a half, has come to increasing prominence. Its ideas have found their way into government policies, funder mandates, and even the economics of scholarly communications. *PLOS ONE* continues to attract a high volume of submissions. Yet the 'old system' of review persists, mentally and in practice, side by side with the new. It could be that we are only at the start of a cascade in which PLOS's arguments will eventually win out. Or perhaps such proposed changes are destined to be a flash-in-the-pan experiment, no more than a brief moment of experiment in the long-evolving history of refereeing and peer review. We do not possess the historical vantage point yet to see this, but we do propose that future projects that wish to enact institutional change within academia and the university can learn from PLOS's radicalism. As we have argued, the lessons PLOS teaches provide both positive guidelines and negative warnings; it is a beacon of change and at the same time a lighthouse of rocks to avoid. And we believe it will remain a good while longer before Reviewer Two absorbs the arguments, strictures, and demands that PLOS makes, lays down, and asks.

References

Adams, Jean, Frances C. Hillier-Brown, Helen J. Moore, Amelia A. Lake, Vera Araujo-Soares, Martin White, and Carolyn Summerbell. 2016. 'Searching and Synthesising "Grey Literature" and "Grey Information" in Public Health: Critical Reflections on Three Case Studies'. *Systematic Reviews* 5 (1): 164. https://doi.org/10.1186/s13643-016-0337-y.

Adema, Janneke. 2018. 'Scholar-Led Publishing: Scaling Small'. Presented at the OpenAIRE workshop, Royal Library, The Hague, The Netherlands, April 5. www.slideshare.net/OpenAIRE_eu/openaire-workshop-beyond-apcs-janneke-adema.

Aktas, Rahime Nur, and Viviana Cortes. 2008. 'Shell Nouns as Cohesive Devices in Published and ESL Student Writing'. *Journal of English for Academic Purposes* 7 (1): 3–14. https://doi.org/10.1016/j.jeap.2008.02.002.

Alberts, Bruce, Brooks Hanson, and Katrina L. Kelner. 2008. 'Reviewing Peer Review'. *Science* 321 (5885): 15. https://doi.org/10.1126/science.1162115.

Aldhous, Peter. 2011. 'Journal Rejects Studies Contradicting Precognition'. New Scientist. May 5, 2011. https://www.newscientist.com/article/dn20447-journal-rejects-studies-contradicting-precognition/.

Allen, Heidi, Alexandra Cury, Thomas Gaston, Chris Graf, Hannah Wakley, and Michael Willis. 2019. 'What Does Better Peer Review Look Like? Underlying Principles and Recommendations for Better Practice'. *Learned Publishing* 32 (2): 163–75. https://doi.org/10.1002/leap.1222.

Allison, Sarah, Ryan Heuser, Matthew Jockers, Franco Moretti, and Michael Witmore. 2011. 'Quantitative Formalism: An Experiment'. Stanford Literary Lab. https://litlab.stanford.edu/LiteraryLabPamphlet1.pdf.

An Open-Source Neural Hierarchical Multi-Label Text Classification Toolkit: Tencent/NeuralNLP-NeuralClassifier. 2019. Python. Tencent. https:// github.com/Tencent/NeuralNLP-NeuralClassifier.

Azoulay, Pierre, Christian Fons-Rosen, and Joshua S. Graff Zivin. 2019. 'Does Science Advance One Funeral at a Time?' *American Economic Review* 109 (8): 2889–920. https://doi.org/10.1257/aer.2 0161574.

Azoulay, Pierre, Joshua S. Graff Zivin, and Gustavo Manso. 2011. 'Incentives and Creativity: Evidence from the Academic Life Sciences'. *The RAND Journal of Economics* 42 (3): 527–54. https://doi.org/10.1111/j.1756-2171.2011.00140.x.

Bakanic, Von, Clark McPhail, and Rita J. Simon. 1989. 'Mixed Messages: Referees' Comments on the Manuscripts They Review'. *The Sociological Quarterly* 30 (4): 639–54.

Baldwin, Melinda. 2017. 'In Referees We Trust?' *Physics Today* 70 (2): 44–9. https://doi.org/10.1063/PT.3.3463.

— 2018. 'Scientific Autonomy, Public Accountability, and the Rise of "Peer Review" in the Cold War United States'. *Isis* 109 (3): 538–58. https:// doi.org/10.1086/700070.

Bardy, A. H. 1998. 'Bias in Reporting Clinical Trials'. *British Journal of Clinical Pharmacology* 46 (2): 147–50. https://doi.org/10.1046/ j.1365-2125.1998.00759.x.

Bar-Ilan, Judit, and Gali Halevi. 2017. 'Post Retraction Citations in Context: A Case Study'. *Scientometrics* 113 (1): 547–65. https://doi .org/10.1007/s11192-017-2242-0.

Batagelj, Vladimir, Anuška Ferligoj, and Flaminio Squazzoni. 2017. 'The Emergence of a Field: A Network Analysis of Research on Peer Review'. *Scientometrics* 113 (1): 503–32. https://doi.org/10.1007/ s11192-017-2522-8.

Baverstock, Alison. 2016. 'Is Peer Review Still the Content Industry's Upper House?' *Learned Publishing* 29 (1): 65–8. https://doi.org/10.1002/leap.1013.

Behar, Ruth, and Deborah A. Gordon, eds. 1995. *Women Writing Culture*. Berkeley: University of California Press.

Belcher, Diane D. 2007. 'Seeking Acceptance in an English-Only Research World'. *Journal of Second Language Writing* 16 (1): 1–22. https://doi.org/10.1016/j.jslw.2006.12.001.

Belluz, Julia. 2015. 'Let's Stop Pretending Peer Review Works'. *Vox*. December 7, 2015. http://www.vox.com/2015/12/7/9865086/peer-review-science-problems.

Berkenkotter, Carol. 1995. 'The Power and the Perils of Peer Review'. *Rhetoric Review* 13 (2): 245–48.

'Berlin Declaration on Open Access to Knowledge in the Sciences and Humanities'. 2003. October 22, 2003. http://oa.mpg.de/lang/en-uk/berlin-prozess/berliner-erklarung.

Beukeboom, Camiel J., and Christian Burgers. 2017. 'Linguistic Bias'. *Oxford Research Encyclopedia of Communication*. https://doi.org/10.1093/acrefore/9780190228613.013.439.

Bhaskar, Michael. 2016. *Curation: The Power of Selection in a World of Excess*. London: Piatkus.

Biernat, Monica, M. , J. Tocci, and Joan C. Williams. 2012. 'The Language of Performance Evaluations: Gender-Based Shifts in Content and Consistency of Judgment'. *Social Psychological and Personality Science* 3 (2): 186–92. https://doi.org/10.1177/1948550611415693.

Blei, David M., Andrew Y. Ng, and Michael I. Jordan. 2003. 'Latent Dirichlet Allocation'. *Journal of Machine Learning Research* (3): 993–1022.

Bolívar, Adriana. 2011. 'Funciones Discursivas de La Evaluación Negativa En Informes de Arbitraje de Artículos de Investigación'. *Núcleo* 23 (28): 59–89.

Bonjean, Charles M., and Jan Hullum. 1978. 'Reasons for Journal Rejection: An Analysis of 600 Manuscripts'. *PS* 11: 480–3.

Bornmann, Lutz. 2011a. 'Peer Review and Bibliometrics: Potentials and Problems'. In *University Rankings: Theoretical Basis, Methodology and Impacts on Global Higher Education*, edited by Jung Cheol Shin, Robert K. Toutkoushian, and Ulrich Teichler, 145–64. Dordrecht: Springer Netherlands. https://doi.org/10.1007/978-94-007-1116-7.

— 2011b. 'Scientific Peer Review'. *Annual Review of Information Science and Technology* 45 (1): 197–245. https://doi.org/10.1002/aris.2011.1440450112.

Bornmann, Lutz, and Hans-Dieter Daniel. 2008. 'The Effectiveness of the Peer Review Process: Inter-Referee Agreement and Predictive Validity of Manuscript Refereeing at Angewandte Chemie'. *Angewandte Chemie International Edition* 47 (38): 7173–8. https://doi.org/10.1002/anie.200800513.

Bornmann, Lutz, Christophe Weymuth, and Hans-Dieter Daniel. 2010. 'A Content Analysis of Referees' Comments: How Do Comments on Manuscripts Rejected by a High-Impact Journal and Later Published in Either a Low- or High-Impact Journal Differ?' *Scientometrics* 83 (2): 493–506. https://doi.org/10.1007/s11192-009-0011-4.

Bourke-Waite, Amy. 2015. 'Innovations in Scholarly Peer Review at Nature Publishing Group and Palgrave Macmillan'. *Insights* 28 (2). https://doi.org/10.1629/uksg.243.

Brainard, Jeffrey, and Jia You. 2018. 'What a Massive Database of Retracted Papers Reveals about Science Publishing's "Death Penalty"'. *Science*. October 25, 2018. www.sciencemag.org/news/2018/10/what-massive-database-retracted-papers-reveals-about-science-publishings-death-penalty.

Brembs, Björn, Katherine Button, and Marcus Munafò. 2013. 'Deep Impact: Unintended Consequences of Journal Rank'. *Frontiers in Human Neuroscience* 7: 1–12. https://doi.org/10.3389/fnhum.2013.00291.

Brown, H. M. 2003. 'Peer Review Should Not Be Anonymous'. *British Medical Journal* 326 (7393): 824. https://doi.org/10.1136/bmj.326.7393.824/b.

Brown, Penelope, and Stephen C. Levinson. 1987. *Politeness: Some Universals in Language Usage*. Cambridge: Cambridge University Press.

Buchanan, James M. 1965. 'An Economic Theory of Clubs'. *Economica* 32 (125): 1. https://doi.org/10.2307/2552442.

Buckheit, Jonathan B., and David L. Donoho. 1995. 'Wavelab and Reproducible Research'. In *Wavelets and Statistics*, edited by Anestis Antoniadis and George Oppenheim, 55–81. Berlin. http://link.springer.com/10.1007/978-1-4612-2544-7_5.

Budden, Amber E., Tom Tregenza, Lonnie W. Aarssen, Julia Koricheva, Roosa Leimu, and Christopher J. Lortie. 2008. 'Double-Blind Review Favours Increased Representation of Female Authors'. *Trends in Ecology & Evolution* 23 (1): 4–6. https://doi.org/10.1016/j.tree.2007.07.008.

Burgers, Christian, and Camiel J. Beukeboom. 2016. 'Stereotype Transmission and Maintenance Through Interpersonal Communication: The Irony Bias'. *Communication Research* 43 (3): 414–41. https://doi.org/10.1177/0093650214534975.

Butchard, Dorothy, Simon Rowberry, Claire Squires, and Gill Tasker. 2017. *Peer Review in Practice*. London: University College London Press. https://doi.org/10.14324/111.9781911307679.15.

Calcagno, V., E. Demoinet, K. Gollner, L. Guidi, D. Ruths, and C. de Mazancourt. 2012. 'Flows of Research Manuscripts Among Scientific

Journals Reveal Hidden Submission Patterns.' *Science* 338 (6110): 1065–9. https://doi.org/10.1126/science.1227833.

Campanario, Juan Miguel. 1993. 'Consolation for the Scientist: Sometimes It Is Hard to Publish Papers That Are Later Highly-Cited.' *Social Studies of Science* 23 (2): 342–62.

— 1996. 'Have Referees Rejected Some of the Most-Cited Articles of All Times?' *Journal of the American Society for Information Science* 47 (4): 302–10. https://doi.org/10.1002/(SICI)1097-4571(199604)47:4<302:: AID-ASI6>3.0.CO;2-0.

— 2009. 'Rejecting and Resisting Nobel Class Discoveries: Accounts by Nobel Laureates.' *Scientometrics* 81 (2): 549–65. https://doi.org/ 10.1007/s11192-008-2141-5.

Campanario, Juan Miguel, and Erika Acedo. 2007. 'Rejecting Highly Cited Papers: The Views of Scientists Who Encounter Resistance to Their Discoveries from Other Scientists.' *Journal of the American Society for Information Science and Technology* 58 (5): 734–43. https://doi.org/ 10.1002/asi.20556.

Casnici, Niccolò, Francisco Grimaldo, Nigel Gilbert, Pierpaolo Dondio, and Flaminio Squazzoni. 2017. 'Assessing Peer Review by Gauging the Fate of Rejected Manuscripts: The Case of the Journal of Artificial Societies and Social Simulation.' *Scientometrics* 113 (1): 533–46. https://doi.org/10.1007/s11192-017-2241-1.

Casnici, Niccolò, Francisco Grimaldo, Nigel Gilbert, and Flaminio Squazzoni. 2017. 'Attitudes of Referees in a Multidisciplinary Journal: An Empirical Analysis.' *Journal of the Association for Information Science and Technology* 68 (7): 1763–71. https://doi.org/10.1002/asi.23665.

Ceci, Stephen J., and Douglas P. Peters. 1982. 'Peer Review: A Study of Reliability.' *Change* 14 (6): 44–8.

Chan, Leslie, Darius Cuplinskas, Michael Eisen, Fred Friend, Yana Genova, Jean-Claude Guédon, Melissa Hagemann, et al. 2002.

'Budapest Open Access Initiative.' February 14, 2002. http://www
.soros.org/openaccess/read.shtml.

Chase, Janet M. 1970. 'Normative Criteria for Scientific Publication.' *The American Sociologist* 5 (3): 262–5.

Chawla, Dalmeet Singh. 2019. 'Thousands of Grant Peer Reviewers Share Concerns in Global Survey.' *Nature*, October 15. https://doi.org/10.1038/d41586-019-03105-2.

Christensen, Clayton M. 1997. *The Innovator's Dilemma: When New Technologies Cause Great Firms to Fail.* The Management of Innovation and Change Series. Boston: Harvard Business School Press.

Chubin, Daryl E., and Edward J. Hackett. 1990. *Peerless Science: Peer Review and U.S. Science Policy.* SUNY Series in Science, Technology, and Society. Albany: State University of New York Press.

Cicchetti, Domenic V. 1991. 'The Reliability of Peer Review for Manuscript and Grant Submissions: A Cross-Disciplinary Investigation.' *Behavioral and Brain Sciences* 14 (1): 119–35.

Coates, Jennifer. 2013. '"So I Mean I Probably . . .": Hedges and Hedging in Women's Talk [2003].' In *Women, Men and Everyday Talk*, 31–49. London: Palgrave Macmillan. https://doi.org/10.1057/97811373149 49_3.

Cockerill, Matthew. 2014. 'Has Open Access Failed?' *OUPblog.* October 23, 2014. https://blog.oup.com/2014/10/open-access-suc cess-failure/.

Collins, Hanry. 2010. 'Interdisciplinary Peer Review and Interactional Expertise.' *Sociologica*, 3: 1–5. https://doi.org/10.2383/33638.

Coniam, David. 2012. 'Exploring Reviewer Reactions to Manuscripts Submitted to Academic Journals.' *System* 40 (4): 544–53. https://doi.org/10.1016/j.system.2012.10.002.

Connor, Ulla, and Anna Mauranen. 1999. 'Linguistic Analysis of Grant Proposals: European Union Research Grants.' *English for Specific*

Purposes 18 (1): 47–62. https://doi.org/10.1016/S0889-4906(97)00026-4.

Costello, Leslie C. 2010. 'Perspective: Is NIH Funding the "Best Science by the Best Scientists"? A Critique of the NIH R01 Research Grant Review Policies'. *Academic Medicine* 85 (5): 775–9. https://doi.org/10.1097/ACM.0b013e3181d74256.

Crompton, Peter. 1997. 'Hedging in Academic Writing: Some Theoretical Problems.' *English for Specific Purposes* 16 (4): 271–87. https://doi.org/10.1016/S0889-4906(97)00007-0.

Cronin, Blaise. 1984. *The Citation Process: The Role and Significance of Citations in Scientific Communication*. London: T. Graham.

— 1998. 'Metatheorizing Citation.' *Scientometrics* 43 (1): 45–55. https://doi.org/10.1007/BF02458393.

— 2000. 'Semiotics and Evaluative Bibliometrics'. *Journal of Documentation* 56 (4): 440–53. https://doi.org/10.1108/EUM0000000007123.

— 2009. 'Vernacular and Vehicular Language'. *Journal of the American Society for Information Science and Technology* 60 (3): 433. https://doi.org/10.1002/asi.21010.

Crotty, Michael. 1998. *The Foundations of Social Research: Meaning and Perspective in the Research Process*. London: Sage Publications.

Da, Nan Z. 2019. 'The Computational Case against Computational Literary Studies'. *Critical Inquiry* 45 (3): 601–39. https://doi.org/10.1086/702594.

Dall'Aglio, Paolo. 2006. 'Peer Review and Journal Models'. *ArXiv*. http://arxiv.org/abs/physics/0608307.

Daniel, Hans-Dieter. 1993. *Guardians of Science: Fairness and Reliability of Peer Review*. Translated by William E. Russey. Weinheim: VCH.

Daniels, Aubrey C. 2009. *Oops! 13 Management Practices That Waste Time and Money (and What to Do Instead)*. Atlanta, GA: Performance Management Publications.

Davies, Christie. 1989. 'Goffman's Concept of the Total Institution: Criticisms and Revisions'. *Human Studies* 12 (1/2): 77–95.

DeCoursey, Thomas. 2006. 'The Pros and Cons of Open Peer Review'. *Nature*. https://doi.org/10.1038/nature04991.

Denzin, Norman K. 2010. 'Grounded and Indigenous Theories and the Politics of Pragmatism'. *Sociological Inquiry* 80 (2): 296–312. https://doi.org/10.1111/j.1475-682X.2010.00332.x.

Dickersin, K., S. Chan, T.C. Chalmers, H.S. Sacks, and H. Smith. 1987. 'Publication Bias and Clinical Trials'. *Controlled Clinical Trials* 8 (4): 343–53. https://doi.org/10.1016/0197-2456(87)90155-3.

Dickersin, Kay, Yuan-I. Min, and Curtis L. Meinert. 1992. 'Factors Influencing Publication of Research Results: Follow-up of Applications Submitted to Two Institutional Review Boards'. *JAMA* 267 (3): 374–8. https://doi.org/10.1001/jama.1992.03480030052036.

Dressen-Hammouda, Dacia. 2013. 'Politeness Strategies in the Job Application Letter: Implications of Intercultural Rhetoric for Designing Writing Feedback'. *ASp. La Revue Du GERAS*, (64): 139–59. https://doi.org/10.4000/asp.3866.

Drvenica, Ivana, Giangiacomo Bravo, Lucija Vejmelka, Aleksandar Dekanski, and Olgica Nedić. 2019. 'Peer Review of Reviewers: The Author's Perspective'. *Publications* 7 (1). https://doi.org/10.3390/publications7010001.

Eisenstein, Elizabeth L. 2009. *The Printing Press as an Agent of Change: Communications and Cultural Transformations in Early-Modern Europe*. Cambridge: Cambridge University Press. https://doi.org/10.1017/CBO9781107049963.

Emerson, Robert M., Rachel I. Fretz, and Linda L. Shaw. 1995. 'Writing Ethnographic Fieldnotes'. *Chicago Guides to Writing, Editing, and Publishing*. Chicago: The University of Chicago Press.

Englander, Karent. 2006. 'Revision of Scientific Manuscripts by Non-Native English-Speaking Scientists in Response to Journal Editors' Language Critiques'. *Journal of Applied Linguistics and Professional Practice* 3 (2): 129–61. https://doi.org/10.1558/japl.v3i2.129.

Enslin, Penny, and Nicki Hedge. 2018. 'On Peer Review as the "Gold Standard" in Measuring Research Excellence: From Secrecy to Openness?' *Journal of Philosophy of Education* 52 (3): 379–96. https://doi.org/10.1111/1467-9752.12312.

Erikson, Martin G., and Peter Erlandson. 2014. 'A Taxonomy of Motives to Cite'. *Social Studies of Science* 44 (4): 625–37. https://doi.org/10.1177/0306312714522871.

Ernst, E., and T. Kienbacher. 1991. 'Chauvinism'. *Nature* 352 (6336): 560. https://doi.org/10.1038/352560b0.

Eve, Martin Paul. 2013. 'Before the Law: Open Access, Quality Control and the Future of Peer Review'. In *Debating Open Access*, edited by Nigel Vincent and Chris Wickham, 68–81. London: British Academy.

— 2017. 'Scarcity and Abundance'. In *The Bloomsbury Handbook of Electronic Literature*, edited by Joseph Tabbi, 385–98. London: Bloomsbury.

— 2019. Close Reading With Computers: Textual Scholarship, *Computational Formalism, and David Mitchell's* Cloud Atlas. Stanford, CA: Stanford University Press.

— 2020. 'Reading Scholarship Digitally'. In *Reassembling Scholarly Communications: Histories, Infrastructures, and Global Politics of Open Access*, edited by Martin Paul Eve and Jonathan Gray. Cambridge, MA: The MIT Press.

Eve, Martin Paul, and Jonathan Gray, eds. 2020. *Reassembling Scholarly Communications: Histories, Infrastructures, and Global Politics of Open Access*. Cambridge, MA: The MIT Press.

Eyre-Walker, Adam, and Nina Stoletzki. 2013. 'The Assessment of Science: The Relative Merits of Post-Publication Review, the Impact Factor, and the Number of Citations'. *PLOS Biology* 11 (10): e1001675. https://doi.org/10.1371/journal.pbio.1001675.

Falagas, Matthew E., Angeliki Zarkali, Drosos E. Karageorgopoulos, Vangelis Bardakas, and Michael N. Mavros. 2013. 'The Impact of Article Length on the Number of Future Citations: A Bibliometric Analysis of General Medicine Journals'. *PLOS ONE* 8 (2): e49476. https://doi.org/10.1371/journal.pone.0049476.

Fanelli, Daniele. 2010. 'Do Pressures to Publish Increase Scientists' Bias? An Empirical Support from US States Data'. *PLoS ONE* 5 (4). https://doi.org/10.1371/journal.pone.0010271.

— 2011. 'Negative Results Are Disappearing from Most Disciplines and Countries'. *Scientometrics* 90 (3): 891–904. https://doi.org/10.1007/s11192-011-0494-7.

Fang, Ferric C., Anthony Bowen, and Arturo Casadevall. 2016. 'NIH Peer Review Percentile Scores Are Poorly Predictive of Grant Productivity'. *ELife* 5 (February). https://doi.org/10.7554/eLife.13323.

Fang, Ferric C., and Arturo Casadevall. 2011. 'Retracted Science and the Retraction Index'. *Infection and Immunity* 79 (10): 3855–9. https://doi.org/10.1128/IAI.05661-11.

Fernández, Eliecer Crespo. 2005. 'Euphemistic Strategies in Politeness and Face Concerns'. *Pragmalingüística* (13): 77–86. https://doi.org/10.25267/Pragmalinguistica.2017.i25.

Fierro, Paula Cabezas del, Omar Sabaj Meruane, Germán Varas Espinoza, and Valeria González Herrera. 2018. 'Peering into Peer Review: Good Quality Reviews of Research Articles Require Neither Writing Too Much nor Taking Too Long'. *Transinformação* 30 (2): 209–18. https://doi.org/10.1590/2318-08892018000200006.

Fish, Stanley. 1988. 'No Bias, No Merit: The Case against Blind Submission'. *PMLA* 103 (5): 739–48.

Fisher, Martin, Stanford B. Friedman, and Barbara Strauss. 1994. 'The Effects of Blinding on Acceptance of Research Papers by Peer Review'. *JAMA* 272 (2): 143–46. https://doi.org/10.1001/jama.1994.03520020069019.

Fitzpatrick, Kathleen. 2011. *Planned Obsolescence: Publishing, Technology, and the Future of the Academy*. New York: New York University Press.

— 2019. *Generous Thinking: The University and the Public Good*. Baltimore, MD: Johns Hopkins University Press.

Fogg, Louis, and Donald W. Fiske. 1993. 'Foretelling the Judgments of Reviewers and Editors'. *American Psychologist* 48 (3): 293–4. https://doi.org/10.1037/0003-066X.48.3.293.

Ford, Emily. 2013. 'Defining and Characterizing Open Peer Review: A Review of the Literature'. *Journal of Scholarly Publishing* 44 (4): 311–26. https://doi.org/10.3138/jsp.44-4-001.

Fortanet, Inmaculada. 2008. 'Evaluative Language in Peer Review Referee Reports'. *Journal of English for Academic Purposes* 7 (1): 27–37. https://doi.org/10.1016/j.jeap.2008.02.004.

Fuller, Steve. 1999. 'Response to the Japanese Social Epistemologists: Some Ways Forward for the 21st Century'. *Social Epistemology* 13 (3–4): 273–302. https://doi.org/10.1080/026917299298600.

Fyfe, Aileen. 2015. 'Peer Review: Not as Old as You Might Think'. *Times Higher Education*. June 25, 2015. https://www.timeshighereducation.com/features/peer-review-not-old-you-might-think.

Fyfe, Aileen, Flaminio Squazzoni, Didier Torny, and Pierpaolo Dondio. 2019. 'Managing the Growth of Peer Review at the Royal Society Journals, 1865–1965'. *Science, Technology, & Human Values* 41 (5): 922–48. https://doi.org/10.1177/0162243919862868.

Gans, Joshua S. 2017. *Scholarly Publishing and Its Discontents*. Ontario: Core Economic Research Ltd.

Gans, Joshua S., and George B. Shepherd. 1994. 'How Are the Mighty Fallen: Rejected Classic Articles by Leading Economists'. *The Journal of Economic Perspectives* 8 (1): 165–79.

George, Richard T. de, and Fred Woodward. 1994. 'Ethics and Manuscript Reviewing'. *Journal of Scholarly Publishing* 25 (3): 133–45.

'Get The Research'. n.d. Accessed August 21, 2019. https://gettheresearch .org/.

Giannoni, Davide Simone. 2008. 'Medical Writing at the Periphery: The Case of Italian Journal Editorials'. *Journal of English for Academic Purposes* 7 (2): 97–107. https://doi.org/10.1016/j.jeap.2008.03.003.

Giles, Jim. 2007. 'Open-Access Journal Will Publish First, Judge Later'. *Nature* 445 (7123): 9. https://doi.org/10.1038/445009a.

Gillespie, Gilbert W., Daryl E. Chubin, and George M. Kurzon. 1985. 'Experience with NIH Peer Review: Researchers' Cynicism and Desire for Change'. *Science, Technology, & Human Values* 10 (3): 44–54. https://doi.org/10.1177/016224398501000306.

Godlee, Fiona. 2002. 'Making Reviewers Visible: Openness, Accountability, and Credit'. *JAMA* 287 (21): 2762. https://doi.org/ 10.1001/jama.287.21.2762.

Godlee, Fiona, Catharine R. Gale, and Christopher N. Martyn. 1998. 'Effect on the Quality of Peer Review of Blinding Reviewers and Asking Them to Sign Their Reports: A Randomized Controlled Trial'. *JAMA* 280 (3): 237–40. https://doi.org/10.1001/jama.280.3.237.

Godlee, Fiona, Jane Smith, and Harvey Marcovitch. 2011. 'Wakefield's Article Linking MMR Vaccine and Autism Was Fraudulent'. *British Medical Journal* 342: c7452. https://doi.org/10.1136/bmj.c 7452.

Goffman, Erving. 1968. *Asylums*. Harmondsworth, UK: Penguin.

Goldacre, Ben. 2011. 'I Foresee That Nobody Will Do Anything about This Problem'. *Bad Science* (blog). April 23, 2011. http://www.badscience.net/2011/04/i-foresee-that-nobody-will-do-anything-about-this-problem/.

Goodman, Steven N. 1994. 'Manuscript Quality before and after Peer Review and Editing at *Annals of Internal Medicine*'. *Annals of Internal Medicine* 121 (1): 11. https://doi.org/10.7326/0003-4819-121-1-199407010-00003.

Gordon and Betty Moore Foundation. 2002. 'Public Library of Science to Launch New, Free-Access Biomedical Journals with $9 Million Grant'. December 17, 2002. www.moore.org/article-detail?newsUrlName=public-library-of-science-to-launch-new-free-access-biomedical-journals-with-$9-million-grant-from-the-gordon-and-betty-moore-foundation.

Gosden, Hugh. 2001. '"Thank You for Your Critical Comments and Helpful Suggestions": Compliance and Conflict in Authors' Replies to Referees' Comments in Peer Reviews of Scientific Research Papers'. *Iberica* 3: 3–17.

— 2003. '"Why Not Give Us the Full Story?": Functions of Referees' Comments in Peer Reviews of Scientific Research Papers'. *Journal of English for Academic Purposes* 2 (2): 87–101.

Greene, Sheila, and Diane Hogan, eds. 2005. *Researching Children's Experience: Methods and Approaches*. Thousand Oaks, CA: SAGE.

Grimaldo, Francisco, Ana Marušić, and Flaminio Squazzoni. 2018. 'Fragments of Peer Review: A Quantitative Analysis of the Literature (1969–2015)'. *PLOS ONE* 13 (2): e0193148. https://doi.org/10.1371/journal.pone.0193148.

Grimaldo, Francisco, Mario Paolucci, and Jordi Sabater-Mir. 2018. 'Reputation or Peer Review? The Role of Outliers'. *Scientometrics* 116 (3): 1421–38. https://doi.org/10.1007/s11192-018-2826-3.

Hames, Irene. 2007. *Peer Review and Manuscript Management of Scientific Journals Guidelines for Good Practice*. Malden, MA: Blackwell.

— 2014. 'The Changing Face of Peer Review'. *Science Editing* 1 (1): 9–12. https://doi.org/10.6087/kcse.2014.1.9.

Hann, Rachel. 2019. 'Interview with Rachel Hann'. *Journal of Arts Writing by Students* 5 (1): 5–12. https://doi.org/10.1386/jaws.5.1.5_1.

Haraway, Donna. 1988. 'Situated Knowledges: The Science Question in Feminism and the Privilege of Partial Perspective'. *Feminist Studies* 14 (3): 575–99. https://doi.org/10.2307/3178066.

Hartley, John. 2015. 'Public Intellectuals: *La Lutte Continue?*' *Media International Australia* 156 (1): 108–22. https://doi.org/10.1177/1329878X1515600113.

Hartley, John, Jason Potts, Lucy Montgomery, Ellie Rennie, and Cameron Neylon. 2019. 'Do We Need to Move from Communication Technology to User Community? A New Economic Model of the Journal as a Club'. *Learned Publishing* 32 (1): 27–35. https://doi.org/10.1002/leap.1228.

Harwood, Nigel. 2005a. '"I Hoped to Counteract the Memory Problem, but I Made No Impact Whatsoever": Discussing Methods in Computing Science Using I'. *English for Specific Purposes* 24 (3): 243–67. https://doi.org/10.1016/j.esp.2004.10.002.

— 2005b. '"Nowhere Has Anyone Attempted . . . In This Article I Aim to Do Just That": A Corpus-Based Study of Self-Promotional I and We in Academic Writing across Four Disciplines'. *Journal of Pragmatics, Focus-on Issue: Marking Discourse*, 37 (8): 1207–31. https://doi.org/10.1016/j.pragma.2005.01.012.

Held, Gudrun. 2010. 'Submission Strategies As an Expression of the Ideology of Politeness: Reflections on the Verbalisation of Social Power Relations'. *Pragmatics* 9 (1): 21–36.

Helmer, Markus, Manuel Schottdorf, Andreas Neef, and Demian Battaglia. 2017. 'Gender Bias in Scholarly Peer Review'. *ELife* 6: e21718. https://doi.org/10.7554/eLife.21718.

Herron, Daniel M. 2012. 'Is Expert Peer Review Obsolete? A Model Suggests That Post-Publication Reader Review May Exceed the Accuracy of Traditional Peer Review'. *Surgical Endoscopy* 26 (8): 2275–80. https://doi.org/10.1007/s00464-012-2171-1.

Hinkel, Eli. 2005. 'Hedging, Inflating, and Persuading in L2 Academic Writing'. *Applied Language Learning* 15: 29–53.

Hirschauer, Stefan. 2010. 'Editorial Judgments: A Praxeology of "Voting" in Peer Review'. *Social Studies of Science* 40 (1): 71–103. https://doi.org/10.1177/0306312709335405.

Holmwood, John. 2020. 'Open Access, "Publicity", and Democratic Knowledge'. In *Reassembling Scholarly Communications: Histories, Infrastructures, and Global Politics of Open Access*, edited by Martin Paul Eve and Jonathan Gray. Cambridge, MA: The MIT Press.

Houghton, John W. 2011. 'The Costs and Potential Benefits of Alternative Scholarly Publishing Models'. *Information Research* 16 (1). http://informationr.net/ir/16-1/paper469.html.

Hudson, Nicholas. 2002. 'Challenging Eisenstein: Recent Studies in Print Culture'. *Eighteenth-Century Life* 26 (2): 83–95.

Huisman, Janine, and Jeroen Smits. 2017. 'Duration and Quality of the Peer Review Process: The Author's Perspective'. *Scientometrics* 113 (1): 633–50. https://doi.org/10.1007/s11192-017-2310-5.

Hyland, Ken. 1996. 'Writing Without Conviction? Hedging in Science Research Articles'. *Applied Linguistics* 17 (4): 433–54. https://doi.org/10.1093/applin/17.4.433.

— 1998. 'Boosting, Hedging and the Negotiation of Academic Knowledge'. *Text – Interdisciplinary Journal for the Study of Discourse* 18 (3): 349–82. https://doi.org/10.1515/text.1.1998.18.3.349.

— 2000. 'Hedges, Boosters and Lexical Invisibility: Noticing Modifiers in Academic Texts'. *Language Awareness* 9 (4): 179–97. https://doi.org/10.1080/09658410008667145.

— 2004. *Disciplinary Discourses: Social Interactions in Academic Writing*. Ann Arbor: University of Michigan Press.

Ingelfinger, Franz J. 1974. 'Peer Review in Biomedical Publication'. *The American Journal of Medicine* 56: 686–92.

Ioannidis, John P. A. 1998. 'Effect of the Statistical Significance of Results on the Time to Completion and Publication of Randomized Efficacy Trials'. *JAMA* 279 (4): 281–6. https://doi.org/10.1001/jama.279.4.281.

Jefferies, Janis, and Sarah Kember. 2019. 'Introduction'. In *Whose Book Is It Anyway? A View from Elsewhere on Publishing, Copyright and Creativity*, edited by Janis Jefferies and Sarah Kember, 1–15. Cambridge, UK: Open Book Publishers.

Jockers, Matthew L. 2013. *Macroanalysis: Digital Methods and Literary History*. Topics in the Digital Humanities. Urbana: University of Illinois Press.

Johns, Adrian. 1998. *The Nature of the Book*. Chicago: The University of Chicago Press.

Justice, Amy C., Mildred K. Cho, Margaret A. Winker, Jesse A. Berlin, Drummond Rennie, and the PEER Investigators. 1998. 'Does Masking Author Identity Improve Peer Review Quality?: A Randomized Controlled Trial'. *JAMA* 280 (3): 240–2. https://doi.org/10.1001/jama.280.3.240.

Kaatz, Anna, Belinda Gutierrez, and Molly Carnes. 2014. 'Threats to Objectivity in Peer Review: The Case of Gender'. *Trends in Pharmacological Sciences* 35 (8): 371–3. https://doi.org/10.1016/j.tips.2014.06.005.

Kahin, Brian, and Hal R. Varian, eds. 2000. *Internet Publishing and Beyond: The Economics of Digital Information and Intellectual Property*. A Publication of the Harvard Information Infrastructure Project. Cambridge, MA: MIT Press.

Kennison, Rebecca. 2016. 'Back to the Future: (Re)Turning from Peer Review to Peer Engagement'. *Learned Publishing* 29 (1): 69–71. https://doi.org/10.1002/leap.1001.

Kim, Loi Chek, and Jason Miin-Hwa Lim. 2015. 'Hedging in Academic Writing – A Pedagogically-Motivated Qualitative Study'. *Procedia – Social and Behavioral Sciences*, 7th World Conference on Educational Sciences, 197: 600–607. https://doi.org/10.1016/j.sbspro.2015.07.200.

Kourilova, M. 1998. 'Communicative Characteristics of Reviews of Scientific Papers Written by Non-Native Users of English'. *Endocrine Regulations* 32 (2): 107–14.

Kravitz, Richard L., Peter Franks, Mitchell D. Feldman, Martha Gerrity, Cindy Byrne, and William M. Tierney. 2010. 'Editorial Peer Reviewers' Recommendations at a General Medical Journal: Are They Reliable and Do Editors Care?' *PLOS ONE* 5 (4): e10072. https://doi.org/10.1371/journal.pone.0010072.

Kvale, Steinar. 1996. *Interviews: An Introduction to Qualitative Research Interviewing*. Thousand Oaks, CA: Sage Publications.

LaFollette, Marcel C. 1992. *Stealing into Print: Fraud, Plagiarism, and Misconduct in Scientific Publishing*. Berkeley: University of California Press.

Lamont, Michèle. 2009. *How Professors Think: Inside the Curious World of Academic Judgment*. Cambridge, MA: Harvard University Press.

Lave, Jean, and Etienne Wenger. 1991. *Situated Learning: Legitimate Peripheral Participation. Learning in Doing*. Cambridge: Cambridge University Press.

Lawrence, Peter A. 2007. 'The Mismeasurement of Science'. *Current Biology* 17 (15): R583–5. https://doi.org/10.1016/j.cub.2007.06.014.

Lillis, Theresa, and Mary Jane Curry. 2015. 'The Politics of English, Language and Uptake: The Case of International Academic Journal Article Reviews'. *AILA Review* 28: 127–50. https://doi.org/10.1075/aila.28.06lil.

Lindner, Mark D., and Richard K. Nakamura. 2015. 'Examining the Predictive Validity of NIH Peer Review Scores'. Edited by Neil R. Smalheiser. *PLOS ONE* 10 (6): e0126938. https://doi.org/10.1371/journal.pone.0126938.

Lindsey, Duncan, and Thomas Lindsey. 1978. 'The Outlook of Journal Editors and Referees on the Normative Criteria of Scientific Craftsmanship: Viewpoints from Psychology, Social Work and Sociology'. *Quality and Quantity* 12 (1): 45–62. https://doi.org/10.1007/BF00138658.

Link, Ann M. 1998. 'US and Non-US Submissions: An Analysis of Reviewer Bias'. *JAMA* 280 (3): 246–7. https://doi.org/10.1001/jama.280.3.246.

Lloyd, Margaret E. 1990. 'Gender Factors in Reviewer Recommendations for Manuscript Publication'. *Journal of Applied Behavior Analysis* 23 (4): 539-43. https://doi.org/10.1901/jaba.1990.23-539.

Lock, Stephen. 1986. *A Difficult Balance: Editorial Peer Review in Medicine*. The Rock Carling Fellowship. Philadelphia, PA: ISI Press.

Lodahl, Janice Beyer, and Gerald Gordon. 1972. 'The Structure of Scientific Fields and the Functioning of University Graduate Departments'. *American Sociological Review* 37 (1): 57. https://doi.org/10.2307/2093493.

Lundh, Andreas, Marija Barbateskovic, Asbjørn Hróbjartsson, and Peter C. Gøtzsche. 2010. 'Conflicts of Interest at Medical Journals: The Influence of Industry-Supported Randomised Trials on Journal Impact Factors and Revenue – Cohort Study'. *PLOS Medicine* 7 (10): e1000354. https://doi.org/10.1371/journal.pmed.1000354.

MacCallum, Catriona J. 2006. 'ONE for All: The Next Step for PLoS'. *PLOS Biology* 4 (11): e401. https://doi.org/10.1371/journal.pbio.00 40401.

Mahoney, Michael J. 1977. 'Publication Prejudices: An Experimental Study of Confirmatory Bias in the Peer Review System'. *Cognitive Therapy and Research* 1 (2): 161–75. https://doi.org/10.1007/BF01173636.

Mandler, Peter. 2013. 'Open Access for the Humanities: Not for Funders, Scientists or Publishers'. *Journal of Victorian Culture* 18 (4): 551–7. https://doi.org/10.1080/13555502.2013.865981.

McCurdy, David W., James P. Spradley, and Dianna J. Shandy. 2005. *The Cultural Experience: Ethnography in Complex Society*. 2nd ed. Long Grove, IL: Waveland Press.

McGuigan, Glenn S., and Robert D. Russell. 2008. 'The Business of Academic Publishing: A Strategic Analysis of the Academic Journal Publishing Industry and Its Impact on the Future of Scholarly Publishing'. *Electronic Journal of Academic and Special Librarianship* 9 (3). http://southernlibrarianship.icaap.org/content/v09n03/mcgui gan_g01.html.

McKenzie, Lindsay. 2019. 'AI That Summarizes Research Papers Could Have Useful Applications for Academics'. *Inside Higher Ed.* May 14, 2019. www.insidehighered.com/news/2019/05/14/ai-summarizes-research-papers-could-have-useful-applications-academics.

McNutt, Robert A., Arthur T. Evans, Robert H. Fletcher, and Suzanne W. Fletcher. 1990. 'The Effects of Blinding on the Quality of Peer Review: A Randomized Trial'. *JAMA* 263 (10): 1371–6. https://doi .org/10.1001/jama.1990.03440100079012.

Meng, Weishi. 2016. 'Peer Review: Is NIH Rewarding Talent?' *Science Transparency*. January 10, 2016. https://scienceretractions .wordpress.com/2016/01/10/peer-review-is-nih-rewarding-ta lent/.

Merriam, Sharan B. 1998. *Qualitative Research and Case Study Applications in Education*. San Francisco, CA: Jossey-Bass Publishers.

Meruane, Omar Sabaj, Carlos González Vergara, and Álvaro Pina-Stranger. 2016. 'What We Still Don't Know About Peer Review'. *Journal of Scholarly Publishing* 47 (2): 180–212. https://doi.org/10.3138/jsp.47.2.180.

Mom, Charlie, Ulf Sandström, and Peter van den Besselaar. 2018. 'Does Cronyism Affect Grant Application Success? The Role of Organizational Proximity'. *STI 2018 Conference Proceedings*, 1579–85.

Montgomery, Lucy, John Hartley, Cameron Neylon, Malcolm Gillies, Eve Gray, Carsten Herrmann-Pillath, Chun-Kai (Karl) Huang, et al. 2018. 'Open Knowledge Institutions'. *Works in Progress*, July. https://doi.org/10.21428/99f89a34.

Moore, Samuel, Cameron Neylon, Martin Paul Eve, Daniel Paul O'Donnell, and Damian Pattinson. 2017. 'Excellence R Us: University Research and the Fetishisation of Excellence'. *Palgrave Communications* 3. https://doi.org/10.1057/palcomms.2016.105.

Moretti, Franco. 2007. *Graphs, Maps, Trees: Abstract Models for Literary History*. London: Verso.

——— 2013. *Distant Reading*. London: Verso.

Morrison, Heather. 2013. 'Economics of Scholarly Communication in Transition'. *First Monday* 18 (6). https://doi.org/10.5210/fm.v18i6.4370.

Moxham, Noah, and Aileen Fyfe. 2018. 'The Royal Society and the Prehistory of Peer Review, 1665–1965'. *The Historical Journal* 61 (4): 863–89. https://doi.org/10.1017/S0018246X17000334.

Mrowinski, Maciej J., Agata Fronczak, Piotr Fronczak, Olgica Nedic, and Marcel Ausloos. 2016. 'Review Time in Peer Review: Quantitative Analysis and Modelling of Editorial Workflows'. *Scientometrics* 107 (1): 271–86. https://doi.org/10.1007/s11192-016-1871-z.

Mrowinski, Maciej J., Piotr Fronczak, Agata Fronczak, Marcel Ausloos, and Olgica Nedic. 2017. 'Artificial Intelligence in Peer Review: How Can Evolutionary Computation Support Journal Editors?' *PLOS ONE* 12 (9): e0184711. https://doi.org/10.1371/journal.pone.0184711.

Mulligan, Adrian, Louise Hall, and Ellen Raphael. 2013. 'Peer Review in a Changing World: An International Study Measuring the Attitudes of Researchers'. *Journal of the American Society for Information Science and Technology* 64 (1): 132–61. https://doi.org/10.1002/asi.22798.

Murray, Dakota, Kyle Siler, Vincent Lariviére, Wei Mun Chan, Andrew M. Collings, Jennifer Raymond, and Cassidy R. Sugimoto. 2018. 'Gender and International Diversity Improves Equity in Peer Review'. *BioRxiv*, August. https://doi.org/10.1101/400515.

Mustaine, Elizabeth Ehrhardt, and Richard Tewksbury. 2008. 'Reviewers' Views on Reviewing: An Examination of the Peer Review Process in Criminal Justice'. *Journal of Criminal Justice Education* 19 (3): 351–65. https://doi.org/10.1080/10511250802476178.

Myers, Greg. 1989. 'The Pragmatics of Politeness in Scientific Articles'. *Applied Linguistics* 10 (1): 1–35. https://doi.org/10.1093/applin/10.1.1.

Nash, Walter. 1990. *The Writing Scholar: Studies in Academic Discourse*. Newbury Park, CA: SAGE Publications.

Neylon, Cameron. 2010. 'It's Not Information Overload, nor Is It Filter Failure: It's a Discovery Deficit'. *Science in the Open*. July 8, 2010. https://cameronneylon.net/blog/it%e2%80%99s-not-information-overload-nor-is-it-filter-failure-it%e2%80%99s-a-discovery-deficit/.

Nicholson, Joshua M., and John P. A. Ioannidis. 2012. 'Research Grants: Conform and Be Funded'. *Nature* 492 (7427): 34–6. https://doi.org/10.1038/492034a.

Nielsen, Michael. 2011. *Reinventing Discovery: The New Era of Networked Science*. Princeton, NJ: Princeton University Press.

Nikolov, Nikola I., Michael Pfeiffer, and Richard H. R. Hahnloser. 2018. 'Data-Driven Summarization of Scientific Articles'. *ArXiv*. http://arxiv.org/abs/1804.08875.

Nosek, Brian A., Jeffrey R. Spies, and Matt Motyl. 2012. 'Scientific Utopia: II. Restructuring Incentives and Practices to Promote Truth Over Publishability'. *Perspectives on Psychological Science* 7 (6): 615–31. https://doi.org/10.1177/1745691612459058.

O'Brien, Anna, Chris Graf, and Kate McKellar. 2019. 'How Publishers and Editors Can Help Early Career Researchers: Recommendations from a Roundtable Discussion'. *Learned Publishing*. https://doi.org/10.1002/leap.1249.

Okike, Kanu, Kevin T. Hug, Mininder S. Kocher, and Seth S. Leopold. 2016. 'Single-Blind vs Double-Blind Peer Review in the Setting of Author Prestige'. *JAMA* 316 (12): 1315–16. https://doi.org/10.1001/jama.2016.11014.

Olbrecht, Meike, and Lutz Bornmann. 2010. 'Panel Peer Review of Grant Applications: What Do We Know from Research in Social Psychology on Judgment and Decision-Making in Groups?' *Research Evaluation* 19 (4): 293–304. https://doi.org/10.3152/095820210X12809191250762.

Pagano, Michele. 2006. 'American Idol and NIH Grant Review'. *Cell* 126 (4): 637–8. https://doi.org/10.1016/j.cell.2006.08.004.

Paltridge, Brian. 2015. 'Referees' Comments on Submissions to Peer-Reviewed Journals: When Is a Suggestion Not a Suggestion?' *Studies in Higher Education* 40 (1): 106–22. https://doi.org/10.1080/03075079.2013.818641.

— 2017. *The Discourse of Peer Review: Reviewing Submissions to Academic Journals*. London: Palgrave Macmillan.

PEERE Consortium. n.d. 'Publications'. https://www.peere.org/category/publications/.

Petty, Richard E., Monique A. Fleming, and Leandre R. Fabrigar. 1999. 'The Review Process at PSPB: Correlates of Interreviewer Agreement and Manuscript Acceptance'. *Personality and Social Psychology Bulletin* 25 (2): 188–203. https://doi.org/10.1177/0146167299025002005.

Pierie, Jean-Pierre E.N., Henk C. Walvoort, and A. John P.M. Overbeke. 1996. 'Readers' Evaluation of Effect of Peer Review and Editing on Quality of Articles in the *Nederlands Tijdschrift Voor Geneeskunde*'. *The Lancet* 348 (9040): 1480–3. https://doi.org/10.1016/S0140-6736(96)05016-7.

Piper, Andrew. 2018. *Enumerations: Data and Literary Study*. Chicago: The University of Chicago Press.

PLOS. 2012. 'New PLOS Look'. *The Official PLOS Blog*. July 23, 2012. https://blogs.plos.org/plos/2012/07/new-plos-look/.

—— 2016a. 'Ethical Publishing Practice'. PLOS ONE. 2016. http://journals.plos.org/plosone/s/ethical-publishing-practice.

—— 2016b. 'Journal Information'. PLOS ONE. 2016. http://www.plosone.org/static/information.

Potts, Jason, John Hartley, Lucy Montgomery, Cameron Neylon, and Ellie Rennie. 2017. 'A Journal Is a Club: A New Economic Model for Scholarly Publishing'. *Prometheus* 35 (1): 75–92. https://doi.org/10.1080/08109028.2017.1386949.

Poynder, Richard. 2006a. 'Interview with Harold Varmus'. *Open and Shut?* (blog). June 5, 2006. https://poynder.blogspot.com/2006/06/interview-with-harold-varmus.html.

—— 2006b. 'Open Access: Stage Two (Interview with Chris Surridge)'. *Open and Shut?*. June 15, 2006. https://poynder.blogspot.com/2006/06/open-access-stage-two.html.

—— 2011. *'PLoS ONE, Open Access, and the Future of Scholarly Publishing'*. https://richardpoynder.co.uk/PLoS_ONE.pdf.

— 2017. 'Has the Open Access Movement Delayed the Revolution?' *Open and Shut?*. October 11, 2017. https://poynder.blogspot.com/2017/10/has-open-access-movement-delayed.html.

— 2019. 'Open Access: Could Defeat Be Snatched from the Jaws of Victory?' https://richardpoynder.co.uk/Jaws.pdf.

Prasithrathsint, Amara. 2015. 'Linguistic Markers and Stylistic Attributes of Hedging in English Academic Papers Written by Native and Non-Native Speakers of English'. *Manusya: Journal of Humanities* 18 (1): 1–22. https://doi.org/10.1163/26659077-01801001.

Puebla, Iratxe, and Deanne Dunbar. 2018. 'Increased Diversity and Inclusion to Ensure Peer Review Quality'. *EveryONE: The PLOS ONE Blog*. September 10, 2018. https://blogs.plos.org/everyone/2018/09/10/peer-review-week-2018-diversity/, http://blogs.plos.org/everyone/?p=22196.

Pullum, Geoffrey K. 1984. 'Stalking the Perfect Journal'. *Natural Language & Linguistic Theory* 2 (2): 261–7.

Rachar, Matthew. 2016. 'Power, Hegemony, and Social Reality in Gramsci and Searle'. *Journal of Political Power* 9 (2): 227–47. https://doi.org/10.1080/2158379X.2016.1191222.

'Retraction Watch'. n.d. Retraction Watch. https://retractionwatch.com/.

Risam, Roopika. 2014. 'Rethinking Peer Review in the Age of Digital Humanities'. *Ada: A Journal of Gender, New Media, and Technology* 4. https://doi.org/10.7264/n3wq0220.

Ross, Joseph S., Cary P. Gross, Mayur M. Desai, Yuling Hong, Augustus O. Grant, Stephen R. Daniels, Vladimir C. Hachinski, Raymond J. Gibbons, Timothy J. Gardner, and Harlan M. Krumholz. 2006. 'Effect of Blinded Peer Review on Abstract Acceptance'. *JAMA* 295 (14): 1675–80. https://doi.org/10.1001/jama.295.14.1675.

Ross-Hellauer, Tony. 2017. 'What Is Open Peer Review? A Systematic Review'. *F1000Research* 6: 588. https://doi.org/10.12688/f1000research.11369.2.

Rothstein, Hannah R. 2014. 'Publication Bias'. In *Wiley StatsRef: Statistics Reference Online*. Oxford: John Wiley & Sons. https://doi.org/10.1002/9781118445112.stat07071.

Rothwell, Peter M., and Christopher N. Martyn. 2000. 'Reproducibility of Peer Review in Clinical Neuroscience'. *Brain* 123 (9): 1964–9. https://doi.org/10.1093/brain/123.9.1964.

Rubin, Herbert J., and Irene Rubin. 1995. *Qualitative Interviewing: The Art of Hearing Data*. Thousand Oaks, CA: SAGE.

Salager-Meyer, Françoise. 1994. 'Hedges and Textual Communicative Function in Medical English Written Discourse'. *English for Specific Purposes* 13 (2): 149–70. https://doi.org/10.1016/0889-4906(94)90013-2.

— 2001. 'This Book Portrays the Worst Form of Mental Terrorism: Critical Speech Acts in Medical English Book Reviews (1940–2000)'. In *Approaches to the Pragmatics of Scientific Discourse*, edited by András Kertész. Metalinguistica 9. Frankfurt am Main: Peter Lang.

Saldaña, Johnny. 2009. *The Coding Manual for Qualitative Researchers*. Los Angeles, CA: Sage.

Saleh, Ahlam A., Melissa A. Ratajeski, and Marnie Bertolet. 2014. 'Grey Literature Searching for Health Sciences Systematic Reviews: A Prospective Study of Time Spent and Resources Utilized'. *Evidence Based Library and Information Practice* 9 (3): 28–50.

Samraj, Betty. 2016. 'Discourse Structure and Variation in Manuscript Reviews: Implications for Genre Categorization'. *English for Specific Purposes* 42: 76–88. https://doi.org/10.1016/j.esp.2015.12.003.

Sandler, Todd, and John Tschirhart. 1997. 'Club Theory: Thirty Years Later'. *Public Choice* (93): 335–55. https://doi.org/10.1023/A:1017952723093.

— 1980. 'The Economic Theory of Clubs: An Evaluative Survey'. *Journal of Economic Literature* 18 (4): 1481–521.

Sandström, Ulf. 2009. 'Cognitive Bias in Peer Review: A New Approach'. In *Proceedings of 12th International Conference on Scientometrics and Informetrics*, 28–31.

Sandström, Ulf, and Martin Hällsten. 2008. 'Persistent Nepotism in Peer-Review'. *Scientometrics* 74 (2): 175–89. https://doi.org/10.1007/s11192-008-0211-3.

Sangster, Catherine. 2008. 'The Work of the BBC Pronunciation Unit in the 21st Century'. *AAA: Arbeiten Aus Anglistik Und Amerikanistik* 33 (2): 251–62.

Santos, Boaventura de Sousa. 2002. 'Para uma sociologia das ausências e uma sociologia das emergências'. *Revista Crítica de Ciências Sociais* (63): 237–80. https://doi.org/10.4000/rccs.1285.

Schmidt, Benjamin. 2012. 'Words Alone: Dismantling Topic Models in the Humanities'. *Journal of Digital Humanities* 2 (1). http://journalofdigitalhumanities.org/2-1/words-alone-by-benjamin-m-schmidt/.

Schroter, Sara, Nick Black, Stephen Evans, James Carpenter, Fiona Godlee, and Richard Smith. 2004. 'Effects of Training on Quality of Peer Review: Randomised Controlled Trial'. *British Medical Journal* 328 (7441): 673. https://doi.org/10.1136/bmj.38023.700775.AE.

Scollon, Ronald, and Suzanne B. K. Scollon. 2001. *Intercultural Communication: A Discourse Approach*. 2nd ed. Language in Society 21. Malden, MA: Blackwell.

Searle, John R. 2010. *Making the Social World: The Structure of Human Civilization*. Oxford: Oxford University Press.

Seeber, Marco, and Alberto Bacchelli. 2017. 'Does Single Blind Peer Review Hinder Newcomers?' *Scientometrics* 113 (1): 567–85. https://doi.org/10.1007/s11192-017-2264-7.

Shatz, David. 1996. 'Is Peer Review Overrated?' *The Monist* 79 (4): 536–63.

— 2004. *Peer Review: A Critical Inquiry*. Issues in Academic Ethics.Lanham, MD: Rowman & Littlefield.

Shehzad, W. 2015. 'How to End an Introduction in a Computer Science Article: A Corpus-Based Approach'. In *Corpus Linguistics Beyond the Word: Corpus Research from Phrase to Discourse*, edited by E. Fitzpatrick, 227–41. Amsterdam: Brill Rodopi. https://brill.com/view/title/30110.

Shirky, Clay. 2008. 'It's Not Information Overload. It's Filter Failure'. In *Web 2.0 Expo*. New York. http://blip.tv/web2expo/web-2-0-expo-ny-clay-shirky-shirky-com-it-s-not-information-overload-it-s-filter-failure-1283699.

Silbiger, Nyssa J., and Amber D. Stubler. 2019. 'Unprofessional Peer Reviews Disproportionately Harm Underrepresented Groups in STEM'. *PeerJ* 7 (December): e8247. https://doi.org/10.7717/peerj.8247.

Siler, Kyle, Kirby Lee, and Lisa Bero. 2015. 'Measuring the Effectiveness of Scientific Gatekeeping'. *Proceedings of the National Academy of Sciences* 112 (2): 360–5. https://doi.org/10.1073/pnas.1418218112.

Sipe, Lawrence R., and Maria Paula Ghiso. 2004. 'Developing Conceptual Categories in Classroom Descriptive Research: Some Problems and Possibilities'. *Anthropology & Education Quarterly* 35 (4): 472–85. https://doi.org/10.1525/aeq.2004.35.4.472.

Skains, R. Lyle. 2019. *Digital Authorship: Publishing in the Attention Economy*. Cambridge: Cambridge University Press.

Smigel, Erwin O., and H. Laurence Ross. 1970. 'Factors in the Editorial Decision'. *The American Sociologist* 5 (1): 19–21.

Smith, R. 1999. 'Opening up BMJ Peer Review'. *British Medical Journal* 318 (7175): 4–5. https://doi.org/10.1136/bmj.318.7175.4.

Smith, Richard. 2006a. 'The Trouble with Medical Journals'. *Journal of the Royal Society of Medicine* 99 (3): 115–19.

— 2006b. 'Peer Review: A Flawed Process at the Heart of Science and Journals'. *Journal of the Royal Society of Medicine* 99 (4): 178–82.

— 2010. 'Classical Peer Review: An Empty Gun'. *Breast Cancer Research* 12 (4): S13. https://doi.org/10.1186/bcr2742.

Spencer-Oatey, Helen, and Peter Franklin. 2009. *Intercultural Interaction: A Multidisciplinary Approach to Intercultural Communication*. Research and Practice in Applied Linguistics. New York: Palgrave Macmillan.

Spezi, Valerie, Simon Wakeling, Stephen Pinfield, Jenny Fry, Claire Creaser, and Peter Willett. 2018. '"Let the Community Decide"? The Vision and Reality of Soundness-Only Peer Review in Open-Access Mega-Journals'. *Journal of Documentation* 74 (1): 137–61. https://doi.org/10.1108/JD-06-2017-0092.

Squazzoni, Flaminio. 2010. 'Peering Into Peer Review'. *Sociologica* (3): 1–27. https://doi.org/10.2383/33640.

Stanfield, John H., and Rutledge M. Dennis, eds. 1993. *Race and Ethnicity in Research Methods*. Sage Focus Editions 157. Newbury Park, CA: SAGE.

Steel, Graham. 2013. 'Publishing Research without Data Is Simply Advertising, Not Science'. *Open Knowledge International Blog*. September 3. http://blog.okfn.org/2013/09/03/publishing-research-without-data-is-simply-advertising-not-science/.

Sternberg, Robert J., Mahzad Hojjat, Melanie G. Brigockas, and Elena L. Grigorenko. 1997. 'Getting In: Criteria for Acceptance of Manuscripts in Psychological Bulletin, 1993–1996'. *Psychological Bulletin* 121 (2): 321–3. https://doi.org/10.1037/0033-2909.121.2.321.

Suber, Peter, Patrick O. Brown, Diane Cabell, Aravinda Chakravarti, Barbara Cohen, Tony Delamothe, Michael Eisen, et al. 2003. 'Bethesda Statement on Open Access Publishing'. http://dash.harvard.edu/handle/1/4725199.

Sugimoto, Cassidy R., and Blaise Cronin. 2013. 'Citation Gamesmanship: Testing for Evidence of Ego Bias in Peer Review'. *Scientometrics* 95 (3): 851–62. https://doi.org/10.1007/s11192-012-0845-z.

Swales, John. 1990. *Genre Analysis: English in Academic and Research Settings*. The Cambridge Applied Linguistics Series. Cambridge: Cambridge University Press.

Swales, John M., and Christine B. Feak. 2000. *English in Today's Research World: A Writing Guide*. Michigan Series in English for Academic & Professional Purposes. Ann Arbor: University of Michigan Press.

Tang, Jingwei. 2013. 'Pragmatic Functions of Hedges and Politeness Principles'. *International Journal of Applied Linguistics and English Literature* 2 (4): 155–60. https://doi.org/10.7575/aiac.ijalel.v.2 n.4p.155.

Tattersall, Andy. 2015. 'For What It's Worth – the Open Peer Review Landscape'. *Online Information Review* 39 (5): 649–63. https://doi.org/10.1108/OIR-06-2015-0182.

Tennant, Jonathan, and Tony Ross-Hellauer. 2019. 'The Limitations to Our Understanding of Peer Review'. *SocArXiv*, August. https://doi.org/10.31235/osf.io/jq623.

Tewksbury, Richard, and Elizabeth Ehrhardt Mustaine. 2012. 'Cracking Open the Black Box of the Manuscript Review Process: A Look Inside *Justice Quarterly*'. *Journal of Criminal Justice Education* 23 (4): 399–422. https://doi.org/10.1080/10511253.2011.653650.

The Editors of *The New Atlantis*. 2006. 'Rethinking Peer Review'. *The New Atlantis*, https://www.thenewatlantis.com/publications/rethinking-peer-review.

Travis, G.D.L., and H.M. Collins. 1991. 'New Light on Old Boys: Cognitive and Institutional Particularism in the Peer Review System'. *Science, Technology, & Human Values* 16 (3): 322–41. https://doi.org/10.1177/016224399101600303.

Tregenza, Tom. 2002. 'Gender Bias in the Refereeing Process?' *Trends in Ecology & Evolution* 17 (8): 349–50. https://doi.org/10.1016/S0169-5347(02)02545-4.

Trudgill, Peter. 2000. *Sociolinguistics: An Introduction to Language and Society*. 4th ed. London: Penguin.

Tsang, Eric W.K. 2013. 'Is This Referee Really My Peer? A Challenge to the Peer-Review Process'. *Journal of Management Inquiry* 22 (2): 166–71. https://doi.org/10.1177/1056492612461306.

Turcotte, Claudine, Pierre Drolet, and Michel Girard. 2004. 'Study Design, Originality and Overall Consistency Influence Acceptance or Rejection of Manuscripts Submitted to the Journal'. *Canadian Journal of Anesthesia/Journal Canadien d'anesthésie* 51 (6): 549–56. https://doi.org/10.1007/BF03018396.

Underwood, Ted. 2017. 'A Genealogy of Distant Reading'. *Digital Humanities Quarterly* 11 (2). http://www.digitalhumanities.org/dhq/vol/11/2/000317/000317.html.

— 2019. *Distant Horizons: Digital Evidence and Literary Change*. Chicago: The University of Chicago Press.

van Arensbergen, Pleun, Inge van der Weijden, and Peter van den Besselaar. 2014. 'The Selection of Talent as a Group Process. A Literature Review on the Social Dynamics of Decision Making in Grant Panels'. *Research Evaluation* 23 (4): 298–311. https://doi.org/10.1093/reseval/rvu017.

van den Besselaar, Peter, Ulf Sandström, and Hélène Schiffbaenker. 2018. 'Studying Grant Decision-Making: A Linguistic Analysis of Review Reports'. *Scientometrics* 117 (1): 313–29. https://doi.org/10.1007/s11192-018-2848-x.

van den Besselaar, Peter, Hélène Schiffbaenker, Ulf Sandström, and Charlie Mom. 2018. 'Explaining Gender Bias in ERC Grant

Selection – Life Sciences Case'. In *STI 2018 Conference Proceedings*, 346–52. Leiden University.

van Rooyen, Susan, Tony Delamothe, and Stephen J.W. Evans. 2010. 'Effect on Peer Review of Telling Reviewers That Their Signed Reviews Might Be Posted on the Web: Randomised Controlled Trial'. *British Medical Journal* 341. https://doi.org/10.1136/bmj.c5729.

van Rooyen, S., F. Godlee, S. Evans, N. Black, and R. Smith. 1999. 'Effect of Open Peer Review on Quality of Reviews and on Reviewers' Recommendations: A Randomised Trial'. *British Medical Journal* 318 (7175): 23–7. https://doi.org/10.1136/bmj.318.7175.23.

Varmus, Harold. 2009. *The Art and Politics of Science*. New York: W.W. Norton & Company.

Varttala, Teppo. 2001. 'Hedging in Scientifically Oriented Discourse: Exploring Variation According to Discipline and Intended Audience'. PhD, Tampere: University of Tampere.

Von Bergen, C. W. Martin S. Bressler, and Kitty Campbell. 2014. 'The Sandwich Feedback Method: Not Very Tasty'. *Journal of Behavioral Studies in Business* 7.

Wakefield, A.J., S.H. Murch, A. Anthony, J. Linnell, D.M. Casson, M. Malik, M. Berelowitz, et al. 1998. 'RETRACTED: Ileal-Lymphoid-Nodular Hyperplasia, Non-Specific Colitis, and Pervasive Developmental Disorder in Children'. *The Lancet* 351 (9103): 637–41. https://doi.org/10.1016/S0140-6736(97)11096-0.

Wang, Qi, and Ulf Sandström. 2015. 'Defining the Role of Cognitive Distance in the Peer Review Process with an Explorative Study of a Grant Scheme in Infection Biology'. *Research Evaluation* 24 (3): 271–81. https://doi.org/10.1093/reseval/rvv009.

Ware, Mark. 2011. 'Peer Review: Recent Experience and Future Directions'. *New Review of Information Networking* 16 (1): 23–53. https://doi.org/10.1080/13614576.2011.566812.

Weller, Ann C. 2001. *Editorial Peer Review: Its Strengths and Weaknesses*. Medford, NJ: Information Today.

Willinsky, John. 2009. 'The Stratified Economics of Open Access'. *Economic Analysis and Policy* 39 (1): 53–70. https://doi.org/10.1016/S0313-5926(09)50043-4.

Wilson, Andrew. 2011. 'Failing to Replicate Bem's Ability to Get Published in a Major Journal'. *Notes from Two Scientific Psychologists*. May 7. http://psychsciencenotes.blogspot.com/2011/05/failing-to-replicate-bems-ability-to.html.

Woods, Peter. 2006. *Successful Writing for Qualitative Researchers*. 2nd ed. London: Routledge.

Yong, Ed. 2012a. 'Nobel Laureate Challenges Psychologists to Clean up Their Act'. *Nature*. https://doi.org/10.1038/nature.2012.11535.

— 2012b. 'A Failed Replication Draws a Scathing Personal Attack from a Psychology Professor'. *Not Exactly Rocket Science*. March 10. http://blogs.discovermagazine.com/notrocketscience/2012/03/10/failed-replication-bargh-psychology-study-doyen/#.VsZpH0Leezc.

— 2012c. 'Replication Studies: Bad Copy'. *Nature* 485 (7398): 298–300. https://doi.org/10.1038/485298a.

— 2012d. 'Nobel Laureate Daniel Kahneman Calls for "Daisy Chain" of Psychology Replications'. Phenomena. October 4, 2012. http://phenomena.nationalgeographic.com/2012/10/04/daniel-kahneman-daisy-chain-replications-priming-psychology/.

Zaharie, Monica Aniela, and Marco Seeber. 2018. 'Are Non-Monetary Rewards Effective in Attracting Peer Reviewers? A Natural Experiment'. *Scientometrics* 117 (3): 1587–609. https://doi.org/10.1007/s11192-018-2912-6.

Zuckerman, Harriet, and Robert K. Merton. 1971. 'Patterns of Evaluation in Science: Institutionalisation, Structure and Functions of the Referee System'. *Minerva* 9 (1): 66–100. https://doi.org/10.1007/BF01553188.

Zwiers, Michael L., and Patrick J. Morrissette. 1999. *Effective Interviewing of Children: A Comprehensive Guide for Counselors and Human Service Workers*. Philadelphia, PA: Accelerated Development.

Acknowledgements

This book would not have been possible without the generous support of too many individuals to name. However, the authors are grateful, in particular, to Veronique Kiermer and Damian Pattinson, both of whom facilitated access to the underlying dataset; to Joerg Heber for valuable comments; and to Jennifer Lin, who worked on the original research proposal. We are extremely grateful to Don Waters, Patricia Hswe, and Michael Gossett at the Andrew W. Mellon Foundation. The authors also wish to thank Gurpreet Singh, who assisted us in technical coordination across the Atlantic. We are grateful also to PLOS as a whole for access to the dataset and for supporting this project.

Funding

This study was funded by the Andrew W. Mellon Foundation under grant #21700692 for which we are most grateful. Martin Paul Eve's work on this project was also supported by a Philip Leverhulme Prize from The Leverhulme Trust grant PLP-2019–023.

LEVERHULME

TRUST _____

About the Authors

Martin Paul Eve is Professor of Literature, Technology and Publishing at Birkbeck, University of London. He holds a PhD from the University of Sussex and is the author of five other books: *Pynchon and Philosophy: Wittgenstein, Foucault and Adorno* (Palgrave, 2014); *Open Access and the Humanities: Contexts, Controversies and the Future* (Cambridge University Press, 2014); *Password [a cultural history]* (Bloomsbury, 2016); *Literature Against Criticism: University English and Contemporary Fiction in Conflict* (Open Book Publishers, 2016); and *Close Reading with Computers: Textual Scholarship, Computational Formalism and David Mitchell's Cloud Atlas* (Stanford University Press, 2019). Martin is a member of the UK English Association's Higher Education Committee and the Universities UK Open Access Monographs Working Group; with support from the Andrew W. Mellon Foundation, he founded the Open Library of Humanities. In 2017, Martin was named as one of *The Guardian*'s five UK finalists for higher education's most inspiring leader, alongside the vice chancellors of Cambridge, Liverpool, and Sheffield Hallam Universities and Oxford's politics professor Karma Nabulsi. In 2018, Martin was awarded the KU Leuven Medal of Honour in the Humanities and Social Sciences. In 2019, he was awarded the Philip Leverhulme Prize. Martin is Principal Investigator on the Reading Peer Review project. https://orcid.org/0000-0002-5589-8511

Robert Gadie is a PhD candidate at University of the Arts London, whose doctoral research focuses on the policy implications of artists' epistemological practice. As Principal Editor for the *Journal of Arts Writing by Students* (2015–19), Robert developed a novel peer review framework to accommodate creative submissions and fostered an international reviewer network of MA and PhD students in the arts.

Samuel A. Moore is a Research Fellow in the Centre for Postdigital Cultures at Coventry University. He has a PhD in Digital Humanities from King's College London and over a decade's experience as a publisher and researcher with a focus on open access and the digital commons. His research and teaching sit at the intersections of information studies, critical theory, and science and technology studies (STS). He is also one of the organisers of the Radical Open Access Collective and blogs at www .samuelmoore.org/.

Cameron Neylon is Professor of Research Communication at the Centre for Culture and Technology at Curtin University, where he co-leads the Curtin Open Knowledge Initiative, a multi-million-dollar project examining the future of universities in a networked world. He is also Director of KU Research and an advocate of open research practice who has worked in research and support areas including chemistry, advocacy, policy, technology, publishing, political economy, and cultural studies. He was a contributor to the Panton Principles for Open Data, the Principles for Open Scholarly Infrastructure, and the altmetrics manifesto. He is a founding board member and past president of FORCE11 and served on the boards and advisory boards of organisations including Impact Story, Crossref, altmetric.com, OpenAIRE, the LSE Impact Blog, and various editorial boards. His previous positions include Advocacy Director at PLOS, Senior Scientist (Biological Sciences) at the STFC, and tenured faculty at the University of Southampton. Along with his earlier work in structural biology and biophysics, his research and writing focus on the culture of researchers; the political economy of research institutions; and how these interact, and collide with, the changing technology environment.

Victoria Odeniyi has a Masters in English Language Teaching (University of Sheffield, UK) and completed her doctoral studies in Applied Linguistics (Canterbury Christ Church University, UK). She was a calibrator on the Reading Peer Review project (Birkbeck, University of London) and a co-researcher on a Developing Educators project at Queen Mary University of London, which investigated academic practices and their impact on learning in the Faculty of Science and Engineering. Currently, Victoria is a senior teaching fellow at UCL Institute of Education, London, where she supervises MA Applied Linguistics, TESOL, and MA English Education students. Victoria is also a committee member for the British Association of Applied Linguistics' Professional Academic and Work-based Literacies Special Interest Group, undertakes peer review regularly, and is an editorial adviser for the *International Journal of Multicultural Education*. Current research and professional interests include academic practice, the sociolinguistics of identity, critical intercultural communication, and ethnographic approaches to research. https://orcid.org/0000–0002-1555–7763.

Daniel Paul O'Donnell is Professor of English at the University of Lethbridge, where he is responsible for teaching courses in medieval English language and literature, digital humanities, and grammar. His research interests focus on the practice of the humanities in the age of open science, digital humanities, and early medieval England. He is Principal Investigator of the Future Commons partnership and the Visionary Cross Project, a data-centric study of the representation of the crucifix in early medieval English art and literature. O'Donnell is past president of FORCE11, Global Outlook::Digital Humanities, Digital Medievalist, and the Text Encoding Initiative. He is the editor-in-chief of *Digital Studies/Le champ numérique*. O'Donnell is chair of the steering committee of the FORCE11 Scholarly Communications Institute (FSCI), which is held each August in Los Angeles.

Shahina Parvin is a PhD candidate in Cultural, Social, and Political Thought at the University of Lethbridge, Alberta, Canada, and Assistant Professor (on study leave) in the Department of Anthropology at Jahangirnagar University, Savar, Dhaka, Bangladesh. Her research interests focus on the questions of gender and power. Until 2016, her research questioned biomedical and health professionals' control over Bangladeshi women's reproductive bodies through the discourses of well-being, freedom, and empowerment. Shahina also significantly contributed to women's scholarship by investigating the impacts of micro-finance banking loans on impoverished Bangladeshi women's lives. In her PhD project, she has explored stories of immigrant racialised women's use of mental health services in Lethbridge, Canada, analysing their stories within a broader discussion of gender, race, imperialism, and regulatory aspects associated with biopsychiatric knowledge. Shahina also worked with ethnic minority people in Bangladesh to examine the ways they became economically, socially, and politically marginalised. Additionally, she has been exploring the political history of impoverished Bangladeshi women's migration to the Gulf countries and their post-immigration vulnerabilities.

Cambridge Elements ≡

Publishing and Book Culture

SERIES EDITOR
Samantha Rayner
University College London

Samantha Rayner is a Reader in UCL's Department of
Information Studies. She is also Director of UCL's Centre for
Publishing, co-Director of the Bloomsbury CHAPTER
(Communication History, Authorship, Publishing, Textual
Editing and Reading) and co-editor of the Academic Book of
the Future BOOC (Book as Open Online Content) with UCL
Press.

ASSOCIATE EDITOR
Leah Tether
University of Bristol

Leah Tether is Professor of Medieval Literature and Publishing
at the University of Bristol. With an academic background in
medieval French and English literature and a professional
background in trade publishing, Leah has combined her
expertise and developed an international research profile in
book and publishing history from manuscript to digital.

ABOUT THE SERIES

This series aims to fill the demand for easily accessible, quality texts available for teaching and research in the diverse and dynamic fields of Publishing and Book Culture. Rigorously researched and peer-reviewed Elements will be published under themes, or 'Gatherings'. These Elements should be the first check point for researchers or students working on that area of publishing and book trade history and practice: we hope that, situated so logically at Cambridge University Press, where academic publishing in the UK began, it will develop to create an unrivalled space where these histories and practices can be investigated and preserved.

Cambridge Elements ≡

Publishing and Book Culture

Academic Publishing

Gathering Editor: Jane Winters

Jane Winters is Professor of Digital Humanities at the School of Advanced Study, University of London. She is co-convenor of the Royal Historical Society's open-access monographs series, New Historical Perspectives, and a member of the International Editorial Board of Internet Histories and the Academic Advisory Board of the Open Library of Humanities.

ELEMENTS IN THE GATHERING

The General Reader and the Academy: Medieval French Literature and Penguin Classics
Leah Tether

The Edited Collection: Pasts, Present and Futures
Peter Webster

Reading Peer Review
Martin Paul Eve, Cameron Neylon, Daniel Paul O'Donnell, Samuel Moore, Robert Gadie, Victoria Odeniyi and Shahina Parvin

A full series listing is available at: www.cambrige.org/EPBC

Printed in the United States
By Bookmasters